The Purpose of Temptation

BY Bob Mumford

Living Happily Ever After
The Purpose of Temptation

The Purpose of Temptation

BOB MUMFORD

FLEMING H. REVELL COMPANY
Old Tappan, New Jersey

Library of Congress Cataloging in Publication Data

Mumford, Bob.
    The purpose of temptation.

    "Adapted from the popular tape series: The
purpose and principle of temptation."
    1. Temptation. I. Title.
BT725.M85   233   73–15622
ISBN 0–8007–0633–1

TO those Christians who have spent unnecessary time in spiritual wilderness due to the lack of understanding of the principles upon which God orders His Kingdom

Contents

Introduction

When the Prophet Hosea cried, "My people perish for *lack* of knowledge" (*see* 4:6), he penetrated the need of God's people of every generation. We *must* be instructed in His ways; we *must* come to understand that God works on given principles.

This book on *Temptation* is designed to examine God's ways and learn His principles of operation. It is *not* a theological discourse on the Garden of Eden. Rather, it is a manual of instruction. Learning these skills can help you understand Bible truths and bring you into God's abundant supply for His children.

Like others, I can testify to a life that has been changed. God's provisions for me in physical, financial, and spiritual realms has been according to His promise. These have not come without an element of struggle, and that is why I share these experiences.

Not long after my rather dramatic conversion to Christ, I

heard about "the land that flows with milk and honey"—symbolic of the promises of plenty given in the Bible. Written in everyday language and punctuated with everyday happenings, these chapters will bring you, step by step, into your own promised land.

I am deeply indebted to a small work by Dietrich Bonhoeffer entitled *Temptation*. It was the beginning of the end of a long personal search. Invaluable editorial assistance has been received from Sarah Ricketts and Janet Baum.

O God, our Father, may You be pleased to use this writing in Your own mysterious way—ministering to those tossed on the stormy sea of temptation. In Jesus' Name, Amen.

Bob Mumford

The Purpose of Temptation

1

Temptation in Perspective

"While you were in New York, I came mighty close to break-ing the promise I gave you about not using the car while you were away," a young man said to his father. "You left the keys on the kitchen counter and I carried them around in my pocket for three days fighting the temptation."

The father smiled. "Son, there's nothing like temptation to show you what you'll do if you are given the opportunity!"

As our Heavenly Father views it, temptation serves an essential purpose in our lives. It shows us *what we are* and *where we stand;* and it plays an important role in *what we will be* in the future. Temptation is a factor in the psycho-logical and spiritual growth process everyone must go through if we are to become mature individuals, capable of living a full and meaningful life.

The function of temptation is always to trigger a choice and provoke a definite stand or action. As in the case of the young man and the car keys, the keys on the kitchen counter presented the temptation that forced him to make a difficult and very important decision. Should he disobey his father and commit an act of irresponsibility which would make it psychologically easier to repeat this kind of choice? or should he—by his obedience—establish the pattern for mature and wise decisions in the future?

Actually, temptation is the dividing line between innocence and awareness. Once you have faced temptation and made your choice of action, you have stepped into a new dimension of reality. If your choice is right—you are blessed. If your choice is wrong—you are burned.

Temptations must come into our experience whether we like it or not. It always presents a lesson to be learned. Our choice demonstrates whether the lesson is learned or if it must be repeated.

We teach our children not to cross the street alone. Temptation comes into play the moment the child is given an opportunity to disobey. There is no one around to see, and the street beckons, promising adventure. The response to temptation will determine if the child can be trusted to play alone near the street in the future.

How we face temptation affects every area of our personal experience. To understand more about the nature of temptation and its definite purpose is of vital importance.

Unfortunately, temptation is one of the most misunderstood words in our language. It is thought of as something to be avoided at all cost—something dangerous that will cause much pain or trouble—or something that will surely lead us into wrongdoing.

Temptation *may* lead to these things, but only if we make the definite choice in that direction. Temptation is not the *cause* of trouble or wrongdoing. It just presents us with a choice. To blame my wrongdoing on temptation ("I wouldn't have done it if I hadn't been tempted!") is as ridiculous as saying, "I wouldn't have gotten a ticket if the light hadn't changed to red just before I got to the intersection."

Who was to blame for the ticket—you or the red light? The light only served to present you with a quick choice: Should I stop and obey the law? or hurry through to save a minute— and make myself liable to face the consequences? The decision was entirely yours.

Understanding *how* temptation functions can help us face it differently—and can change our lives. When we Christians are honest with ourselves, we are forced to admit that there is a noticeable discrepancy between the Christian life as we experience it, and what we—down deep in our hearts—hope it can be. I say *hope*, because some of us aren't even sure that the Christian life *can* be much different.

The discrepancy between the beautiful promises in the Bible and the lives of many Christians is explained by some who say that the beautiful promises only refer to heaven. This is termed pie-in-the-sky religion, and it doesn't do much to help us solve our problems here and now. Paul refused this kind of escapism when he emphasized the *now* aspect of the Christian life in Romans 5:17:

The sin of this one man, Adam, caused *death to be king over all*, but all who will take God's gift of forgiveness and acquittal are *kings of life* because of this one man, Jesus Christ.

Real Christianity is when Bible promises become reality. This is how it was meant to be. An overabundance of God's promises (without realizing their provisions) brought me to a place where I refused to seek or accept another biblical promise until the ones I already knew became functional.

Knowing all the promises in the Bible by memory doesn't

make the provisions automatically ours. I know Christians who go around quoting, "So there is now no condemnation awaiting those who belong to Christ Jesus" (Romans 8:1). Yet, they live under constant condemnation, as if they must carry the guilt of their old sins with them to the grave. I know others who quote Scriptures about having joy in their hearts—and they are the saddest, most joyless creatures I have ever met! Still others know all the Scriptures telling how we can love each other. However, they live in marriages that are on the verge of breakup, are unable to communicate love to their own children, and have continual difficulties in business relationships.

Can God heal the brokenhearted—effect recovery to the sick—bring love to the lonely and bitter—save the lost—set free those who are in misery—repair broken relationships? *Can* He bring love, joy, and laughter into gray empty lives— make families one in love and spirit? *Can* He meet your particular need—answer your particular prayer—fulfill the particular promise which you have cherished for years? *Can He—or can't He?* Is the Bible true or is it a bunch of fairy tales—just something to comfort us in this world of problems? Is religion a crutch for the weak who cannot face reality?

I believe firmly that the Bible is true—every word of it; and I have seen enough of those promises turned into real provision over the last years to *know*—without the least doubt —that behind the words of the Bible stands our all-powerful and loving Father, who not only *can* make His words good, but *wants* to see this happen!

So, why aren't we all experiencing the promises of God turned into actual provisions? If the promises are real enough, could there be something else wrong? We must acknowledge there is "something else." In our search for the culprit, we are usually required to turn the searchlight on ourselves. It isn't that we need to pray more, give more time to Bible study, go to more prayer meetings, try harder to "be good," or give more money to missions. All of these things are profitable, but they aren't at the heart of this particular problem which needs to be solved.

Between us and the fulfillment of God's beautiful promises always lies a situation containing temptation—*and it is how we respond to temptation that determines whether or not we receive the fulfillment of our promise.*

In other words, when we learn how to face temptation, we will have learned how to see a promise become reality—ours in personal possession and fulfillment.

Before we go on, we should make very clear what temptation *is not.* I don't want to create another misunderstanding by implying that the reason we don't receive God's provision is because we are repeatedly indulging in sinful acts—like stealing, lying, committing adultery. We can certainly be tempted to do some of these things, and if we choose that sort of life, this would be part of the reason why we are left standing with an empty promise instead of a fulfilled provision. But temptation is more than the comic-book caricature of a sexy woman luring her prey into adultery.

The Greek word which we translate as *temptation* in the Bible, means *that which puts us to the proof—whether by good or malicious design.* Temptation is designed to bring out what is really in our hearts. Temptation, in itself, is not good or evil; it simply puts to the proof and test. This reveals what we really are!

For example, steel must be tempered by heat and put to the test under varying degrees of stress to see how it will react for its intended use. Temptation puts to the test how we will react in a situation related to the promise God has given us. If we react according to biblical specifications, the provision will be ours. It is *not* earned or deserved—because

God's gifts are always free; but the question is whether or not we *have the capacity to receive what God has promised.*

Untempered steel, given too much pressure, will break. Fulfillment of a promise, without preparation, can break us as well. Can you see there is reason for temptation? Its purpose is not to make life hard or difficult, but rather to assist in the preparation needed to receive the good things God desires to give.

Seen in this perspective, temptation isn't something frightening or to be avoided. Rather, it is a necessary part of our Christian lives—something we should understand and face eagerly and joyfully. After all, *temptation is designed to prepare us to receive what we long to have.*

The Bible is our textbook. We will find as we search its pages that the purpose and principle of temptation is clearly revealed and demonstrated here—beginning with the Old Testament and carrying on through the New Testament. A series of test cases will show how temptation provided the turning point which determined the success or failure of experiencing fulfilled promises.

The Christian life can never be defined in *methods.* We can never discover a formula for *how* to face temptation and thus receive the fulfillment of God's promises. However, we will discover that God always operates according to clearly defined principles. When we understand these principles and learn to apply them in our lives, we can move on and grow up into the fullness of life as the Bible presents it.

Right now—before we go any further—why not ask God to open your own understanding to this exciting possibility, and say with me,

Lord, teach me Thy ways.

2

Conditional Promises

Between us and the fulfillment of each of God's promises stands a situation that includes temptation. Let's take a closer look at some of the basic promises God offers all who come to Him and see at what point—in relation to the promise—temptation enters the picture.

Nothing is sadder, in my opinion, than Christians who have resigned themselves to the erroneous idea that God either cannot or will not pour out His blessings on us today. To hear some Christians talk, you would think God a tight-fisted miser who only dribbles out enough blessings to keep us going in this present world; or that He is unfair, raining riches on some and not on others—healing some and not others—according to His inscrutable whim.

The Bible pictures God as eager and anxious to give good things without preference or partiality. While the Bible is often referred to as a Book of Promises, it is just as much a textbook on *How to Turn Promises Into Provisions*. No promise in the entire Bible is an empty promise. Luke 1:37 tells us, "For with God nothing is ever impossible, and no word from God shall be without power or impossible of fulfillment" (AMPLIFIED).

Our first test case is the Israelites, God's chosen people. He brought them out of Egyptian slavery in order to bring them into a land flowing with milk and honey. His promise was, ". . . you will become a great nation in a glorious land 'flowing with milk and honey' even as the God of your fathers promised you . . . God will give you great cities full of good things—cities you didn't build, wells you didn't dig, and vineyards and olive trees you didn't plant . . ." (see Deuteronomy 6:3, 10, 11).

Remember, that although we are speaking of a specific people in a certain place and time in history, the same promises are applicable to us today—as spiritual Israelites. God desires to bring us out of whatever bondage we may be in —psychological, spiritual, or physical—in order to bring us into "a land flowing with milk and honey." This is a picture of the abundance of good things (both spiritual and physical) that He has for us in this life.

It sounds almost too good to be true, doesn't it? God wants to give us everything we could possibly need—things for which we are not required to labor! Moses goes on to say to the Israelites, "God will drive your enemies out before you" (see v. 19).

In plain, everyday language, this means that God desires to lead us into a situation—spiritual *and* physical—where He will provide for our every need—job, home, friends, clothes, food, peace of mind—everything our hearts may desire. To get all of this we do not have to work for it—earn it—or deserve it.

If it is all that simple, why didn't the Israelites move on

into the Promised Land? You and I know the Bible well
enough to be somewhat familiar with their story. They wandered in the wilderness for forty years—grumbling and
complaining all the way; and the entire first generation of
ex-slaves (with two notable exceptions—Joshua and Caleb)
died in the wilderness before their children were able to
enter the land.

Also—if it is all that simple—why aren't you and I dwelling
in our own promised land right now? Instead, we may be
wandering around in our own private wildernesses, probably
doing our share of grumbling and complaining! And some
of us are even likely to die there, without ever coming into
the good life God has promised to us.

First of all, let us take another look at the promise made to
the Israelites. We quite often make the common mistake
that these people seem to have made—that of lifting the
promise out of its surrounding and supporting framework.
Reading Deuteronomy again, we see:

> . . . If you obey these commands you will become a great
> nation in a glorious land "flowing with milk and honey,"
> even as the God of your fathers promised you . . . listen,
> Jehovah is our God, Jehovah alone. You must love him with
> all your heart, soul and might. And you must think con-
> stantly about these commandments I am giving you today.
> You must teach them to your children and talk about them
> when you are at home or out for a walk; at bedtime and the
> first thing in the morning . . . When the Lord your God has
> brought you into the land he promised your ancestors . . .
> when he has given you great cities full of good things—
> cities you didn't build, wells you didn't dig, and vineyards
> and olive trees you didn't plant—and when you have eaten
> until you can hold no more, then beware lest you forget the
> Lord who brought you out of . . . slavery. When you are

full, don't forget to be reverent to him and to serve him and
to use his name alone to endorse your promises . . . You
must not provoke him and try his patience . . . . [King
James Version says it this way: Ye shall not tempt the Lord
your God . . . .] If you obey him all will go well for you
and you will be able to go in and possess the good land
which the Lord promised . . . You will also be able to
throw out all the enemies living in your land, as the Lord
agreed to help you do.

Deuteronomy 6:3–19

The promises sound a little different when they are placed
in the right context, don't they? Listen to another promise
made in Isaiah 1:19: "If you will only let me help you, if you
will only obey, then I will make you rich!" King James Version expresses this same verse: "If ye be willing and obedient,
ye shall eat of the good of the land."

What is God saying? Do you notice some *if* openings in
these statements? In the case of Moses' reminding the Israelites of God's promises, he speaks of "obey these commands." These are the commandments given to Moses by
God—the Ten Commandments. We might capsule his ad-
monition and say, "Obey the commandments, love God
with all your heart, soul and might, teach this to your children, and when you come into the good land and have
eaten your fill, don't forget who gave it all to you; don't
provoke or tempt God. Obey Him and He will chase out your
enemies before you so that you can possess the land. Be
willing and obedient, and you may eat of the good of the
land, you will prosper and be rich."

How do we reconcile these two thoughts? On one hand
God says He wants to give us good things which we do not
have to earn or we do not deserve. On the other hand, He
says we can't have the good provisions *unless* we do certain

things. Is this consistent? And, even more important, is it consistent with the New Testament which tells us that God *gave* His only Son, Jesus Christ, as a free gift—and that by accepting Him as our Saviour we no longer have to pay for our own sins with the death penalty? Instead of a death penalty, we are told we can receive the gift of God's grace, His pardon, and eternal life in Christ.

This brings us to what is probably one of the most debated aspects of the Christian life: legalism versus "everything by grace." There are groups of believers on both sides of the fence—those who lean to the legalistic by overemphasizing the belief that we must observe certain rules and regulations in order to be in right standing with God—and those who say that under the New Covenant (the covenant sealed by Jesus Christ on the cross), we cannot earn God's gifts by keeping rules and regulations. All things are free in Christ.

Must we choose up sides and come out fighting? God forbid! Neither extreme position is correct. Yet both have caught some aspect of the truth and carried it too far. Error may come by emphasis or neglect. God doesn't want legalism but neither does He want disobedience! In reality, everything God has for us is a gift. We cannot earn anything by our own goodness or efforts; however, God's gifts can only be received on certain conditions.

Just in case this sounds like double-talk to you, we shall look at some promises in the New Testament.

"If you stay in me and obey my commands, you may ask any request you like, and it will be granted!" (John 15:7). This is Jesus Himself speaking, and He is giving a remarkable promise. But notice the *if*—there is a condition to the promise. In fact, I don't know of a single promise in the Bible that does not have a condition attached to it.

Consider the promise of salvation: "God loved the world so much that he gave his only Son so that anyone who believes in him shall not perish but have eternal life" (John 3:16). Some people in this world are perishing because they haven't met the condition for salvation, which is offered as a free gift, only to those who choose to believe. The Amplified Bible explains the term *believing* as, "anyone who trusts, clings to, relies on Jesus Christ." We are talking about more than lip service here; rather it is a matter of a total personal trust and reliance on Christ in every aspect of life. That is the condition.

The condition always describes *how* a promise is to be fulfilled. Only under these prescribed conditions can the promise become reality. Taking another promise of Jesus, we note: "I am the Vine, you are the branches. Whoever lives in me and I in him shall produce a large crop of fruit" (John 15:5, 6). The promise is that we shall produce a large crop of fruit, *provided* we live in Him and allow Him to live in us. Jesus goes on to explain *why* this is so. "For apart from me you can't do a thing. If anyone separates from me, he is thrown away like a useless branch, withers and is gathered into a pile with all the others and burned." The reason the condition is necessary is a very simple one—apart from Jesus Christ we cannot produce spiritual fruit!

The reasons for putting conditions on the promises given to the Israelites were the same: apart from God they would not be able to possess the land and enjoy the kind of life God wanted for them. Can you see that giving the condition, "If you are willing and obedient . . ." before the promise, ". . . you will eat of the good of the land . . . ," was due to the fact that God knew if they tried to do it in their own way, they would fail miserably in the end? Their obedience to God was designed to reduce their dependency on their own resources and strength, and increase their dependency on God.

God is not a tyrant who wants us all to cower in obedience before Him; but it is because He loves us and knows our natures well enough to see that—left to our own devices— we always make a mess of things. When Jesus said, "On your own, apart from Me, you can do nothing" (*see* John 15:5), He meant that apart from Him we cannot do anything truly worthwhile and lasting. We just cannot produce the kind of fruits He can produce in us and through us when we stay close to Him and depend on Him. We need to give up our self-sufficiency so that we can come to a place in our Christian experience where we cease from our own frantic labor and let *Him* do the work.

Another truth that Jesus tried to impress on His disciples was that *if they believed in Him,* they would one day do greater works than He was doing. One day the disciples asked Jesus, "What are we to do that we may [habitually] be working the works of God?—What are we to do to carry out what God requires?" Jesus replied, "This is the work (service) that God asks of you, that you believe in the One Whom He has sent—that you cleave to, trust, rely on and have faith in His Messenger" (John 6:28, 29 AMPLIFIED). Jesus said to them—and is saying to us today—that when we stop trying to do things in our own strength and recognize our own insufficiency, then we can let Him work through us.

As Christians, we *know* in our hearts that what we do in our own strength "for the Lord" amounts to zero. We may busy ourselves building churches, organizing missions, revivals, Sunday school rallies. But *we* cannot save anyone. *We* cannot heal anybody. *We* cannot comfort the brokenhearted, give sight to the blind, or set anybody free from the prison of their guilt. It is only when we come to a position of total reliance on Jesus—total trust, obedience and rest from our own labors—that we will see Jesus bring salvation to others through us; see Him heal and comfort others and set them free through us. Always it is *His* doing through our willingness and obedience to *His* command.

This is the *only* way we can ever enter our promised land. Because the promised land is a place of rest, frantic self-efforts do not belong there. Hebrews describes God's promise about a place of rest and how we may enter:

> Although God's promise still stands—his promise that all may enter his place of rest—we ought to tremble with fear because some of you may be on the verge of failing to get there after all. For this wonderful news—the message that God wants to save us—has been given to us just as it was to those who lived in the time of Moses. But it didn't do them any good because they didn't believe it. They didn't mix it with faith. For only we who believe God can enter into his place of rest . . . This new place of rest he is talking about does not mean the land of Israel that Joshua led them into. If that were what God meant, he would not have spoken long afterwards about "today" being the time to get in. So there is a full complete rest still *waiting* for the people of God . . . Let us do our best to go into that place of rest, too, being careful not to disobey God as the children of Israel did, thus failing to get in.   Hebrews 4:1–11

Some people may teach that this place of rest is where we enter after death, but I do not find this consistent with the teachings of Jesus. He said—over and over again—that we are to cease from our own labors *now*, letting Him work through us. Our promised land today is a place of rest where we will dwell in cities we didn't build and receive good things for which we did not work—*because God alone will do the work for and through us.* It is physically and spiritually impossible for Him to do this until we surrender our attempt to do it for ourselves.

The condition God gives us is that we must be willing to give up our own ways and work, and be obedient to His every command as He lives in and works through us. God's promises *must* be seen in relation to their conditions.

It is in the midst of our reaction to the conditions that temptation enters the picture. *Temptation relates to the promise through the condition.* When a promise is given with a condition, God is saying, "I will do this *if* you will do that." Temptation then presents us with the choice either (1) to fulfill God's condition, or, (2) to ignore it. If we fulfill the condition, we can enter into the provision—the promised land. If we ignore the condition, we will not be able to receive fulfillment of the promise.

Returning to Hebrews, we hear:

"But," God says, "I was very angry with them, for their hearts were always looking somewhere else instead of up to me, and they never found the paths I wanted them to follow." Then God, full of this anger against them, bound himself with an oath that he would never let them come to his place of rest.   Hebrews 3:10, 11

God's promises are *real;* so are His conditions. There is still a promised land waiting for you and me. The decision to go there becomes an individual choice. Don't be afraid to venture out into God's provision—your promised land!

3

The Wilderness Complex

Why does God place a "wilderness area" between us and our promised land? For the Israelites, it was a geographical fact that the wilderness existed between the Red Sea and Canaan, their biblical Promised Land. They could not get to Canaan except through the wilderness. For us, the wilderness is not a geographic fact; nevertheless, it is there—a very real wilderness! Between the promise and its actual fulfillment lies a physical and spiritual wilderness, consisting of problems, difficulties, and confusion. This is, of course, the area where temptation enters as a focal point.

We have seen that temptation relates to the promise through the condition. It is in the wilderness that we come to the point of questioning the validity of the condition, and at times the promise itself. That kind of question *must* be solved before we can move on into the provision—and God placed the wilderness experience in our way to bring about

that confrontation. We *must* come to see the validity of His conditions and fulfill them before we can move on.

This may sound extremely serious and definite to some of us who like to think that God's love is of such a nature that He won't hold back the fulfillment of a promise just because the condition isn't completely met. We may ask, "Didn't Jesus take care of all that when He died for us? Didn't Jesus pay our debts and fulfill our conditions so that all we have to do is ask and receive? If we love Him and say our prayers, He will surely give us the promises we have claimed and hung onto for all these years."

If this has been your thinking, you may be in danger of making a serious mistake. The promises you are waiting for may never become yours. I am convinced that if it were at all possible, God would unconditionally give us everything for which we ask. But He cannot, because if He did, it would destroy us.

John D. Rockefeller once said, in essence: "I have seldom, if ever, found a place where I could give in substantial amounts without hurting people." If John D. Rockefeller felt like that, how do you think God feels?

When I first read God's promise of the land flowing with milk and honey—the land with wells, vineyards, cities that I need not labor for—a land just waiting for me—I said, "Lord, that is just wonderful! I'm willing and obedient and ready for it!"

Then, in a way God often speaks to me, my impression was, "No, son, you're not!"

My reply was, "Why not?"

And His answer came, "Son, the one thing you cannot stand right now is success."

But I argued, "Why, Lord! Me? I *can* stand it. Give me my inheritance right now."

To which the Lord asked, "You mean like the prodigal son?"

How did the prodigal son get into trouble? By demanding his inheritance too soon! When all that money was in his pocket, he forgot about his father. Too much—too soon—this nearly destroyed him, and it will do the same to us. (*See* Proverbs 20:21 AMPLIFIED.)

Have you ever watched an instant movie star be "born"? Overnight she is chosen by the star makers, given the Madison-Avenue treatment, television, magazines, parties, attention, and admiration. Soon she becomes a self-willed and self-centered individual. Before long, she is so conceited no one can work with her. Like a shooting star falling from the sky, she shines brilliantly for a season and is burned up, cast away—and forgotten. This may be an extreme example, but watch the pattern in any area where someone comes into sudden success or riches. A million-dollar inheritance can destroy a person who is immature and unprepared. You don't place your son as head of your business when he's fifteen; you give him a job as clean-up boy, and as he proves himself capable, you give him more responsibility.

This is true with material possessions and with spiritual riches, as well. Our Heavenly Father wants us to become spiritually-mature individuals. He wants us to be His witnesses in all the world. He wants to preach powerful sermons through us—do miracles—to show His power and love through us. He cannot, however, dump the whole package on us before we are mature enough to handle the responsibility.

What do you think would happen to me if a wealthy man said, "Mumford, I think you're the greatest teacher I have ever heard. You are doing a marvelous work for the Lord. I'm going to send you five thousand dollars a month for the rest of your life—install you and your family in a new beach-front villa—and give you a new chauffeur-driven Cadillac every year."

I can tell you what would happen, because I know my heart. I would start thinking, "My, I'm really quite a guy. God is pretty lucky to have me around." I would soon forget that God is the source of everything I am and have, and start thinking *I* was the reason things were going so well.

Moses warned the Israelites about four things that could happen when they had received riches and eaten until they were full. Do these have relevance for us today?

(1) They could easily forget God.
(2) They could attribute their good life to a source other than God.
(3) They could provoke God by trying His patience.
(4) They could test and tempt Him.

It is a fairly simple matter to see how one could easily forget God or attribute success to a source other than God when success and riches come our way. A businessman who makes it to the top of his profession, or a politician who wins a landslide election, can be tempted to think it all happened because he did a good job or was a great man.

But, how do we provoke God? The Israelites did it by *asking for more than God wanted them to have at the moment.* They wanted a sign greater than He was pleased to give. This is a temptation that we are also faced with when things prosper for us.

Young Christians, excited over their new-found faith—convinced that God can and will do anything they ask—often go around looking for a situation where they can demonstrate the power of God to others.

This happened to me. During my first year in Bible college, I began to understand a little of the Scriptures concerning divine healing. I was convinced that God could heal anyone—anytime! Once on a student-minister assignment to a church near the college, I found myself face to face with a man in a wheelchair. He had been sick for many years. Eager to see God's power manifested, I stepped over to the man, commanding in a strong voice, "In the name of Jesus, be healed, and stand up!" Nothing happened. I was crushed, of course; and the man, whose hopes had soared for an instant, felt his faith shaken.

In my immaturity I had rushed ahead, asking for a miracle, a sign that God had in no way indicated He wanted to perform right then and there. God can heal. I have seen His healing power at work in many instances. But, at that particular time I had fallen for the temptation to test God. Had He healed the man at that time—not because of my faithfulness and obedience—but because He desired to heal him, I would probably have swelled in pride over my "spirituality," seeing myself as MUMFORD—THE MIRACLE MAN. I would have been in far greater danger of destroying myself and others than before the incident.

When those who receive riches—material or spiritual—consequently stumble and fall, it isn't because the riches in themselves are dangerous or destructive, but because *those who receive them are not prepared to handle them.*

A ten-speed bike is a wonderful gift and so is an electric handsaw. Have you ever seen a youngster go over a curb on his new ten-speed, getting badly bruised? or heard of a fellow who cut off his finger with his new powerful saw? Have you seen a family come into sudden prosperity and shortly thereafter their children run wild on their new motorbikes, get failing grades in school, the marriage goes on the rocks, and the wife runs off with another man? What is your reaction?

You could say, "Ten-speeds and electric handsaws are dangerous—I'll never have any. Prosperity leads to misery. I hope I never get rich." Or do you say, "I can see it takes skill to operate a ten-speed and an electric handsaw. I better learn how to handle such things before I get one. Prosperity must be handled carefully. I better start learning responsible stewardship so that I am prepared if God wants to trust me with more possessions in life."

The first reaction—"I'll never ride a ten-speed . . ."—springs from something I call the *wilderness complex.* We have watched others get hurt by a measure of success, and so we think we are safer while we're poor and in need. I have watched some of my contemporaries rise to fame and position in the church and later fail. As a result, I developed a full-grown wilderness complex. I honestly feared success and was afraid that if it came to me I would forget God, get big-headed, and stumble. "Lord, just keep me broke and humble, half-sick, and driving an old car so that I'll stay dependent on You—and faithful. But don't bless me, Lord. I know I couldn't stand it!"

The Israelites wandered in endless circles in their wilderness. They experienced wonderful miracles from God, ate their fill—and promptly forgot God—or tried His patience by asking for more. Over and over again they repeated the same pattern. Consequently, their wilderness experience was a series of problems with no satisfactory solutions. We see some disastrous consequences come to our contemporary wilderness-wanderers, and conclude that we don't want any blessings. We decide we'd rather stay in a condition of continuous need so that we won't forget our constant dependency on God.

As a part of the wilderness complex, we have developed the idea that success always spoils, power always corrupts, riches are the root of evil. We've become so used to dwelling in the wilderness that we think God wants us to remain there permanently. We accept the wilderness as the only normal way of life for a spiritual Christian.

We reason: Jesus was poor and rode into Jerusalem on a borrowed donkey. So we say it is Christlike to be poor. We extend that thought even further and say it is Christlike and spiritual to suffer constant duress, sickness, financial problems, persecutions, and hardships. We say we can best glorify God by going through these difficulties in order for others to see our patience and conclude that God enables us to bear our burdens without complaining. Permanent wilderness-dwellers look critically at those who appear to live happily in a life free from obvious problems and say, "Just wait—God will deal with you and you will come to understand the serious reality of this life in our sin-sick world.

Suffering will come to you, too. Then you will understand what it is all about and become really spiritual like the rest of us who are called upon to suffer."

This is a form of self-imposed martyrdom that serves to keep you just as far removed from the fulfillment of God's promises as if you were outwardly rebellious and arrogantly disobedient to God's commands. *To take pride in suffering and poverty* is just as disastrous as *taking pride in accumulated riches or a high position.*

Can you see that those Christians who measure their spirituality by their humble station in life are just as much in error as those who say that God always goes first class? The latter measure their spirituality by how much God provides for them. This tendency is called *success ethics*. The two extremes—the wilderness complex and those who run in the prosperity pack—are both wrong. Spirituality, or closeness to God, cannot be measured by either the presence or absence of material and spiritual blessings.

I once had a friend who sincerely wanted to serve God as a missionary to the poorest of Indians. For years he lived in very poor circumstances, giving away everything he received. But instead of sending him to the mission field where he could continue to live in abject poverty, God sent this man to a very prosperous church in a wealthy suburb. There he had to minister to the champagne-and-jet-set crowd. My friend was deeply disturbed about the situation. He didn't consider it proper to serve God in such luxurious surroundings. He found himself unable to cope with the turn of events until God impressed upon him: "For many years you have been more than willing to adjust your standard of living down to suffer with the poor. Now I am asking you to adjust your standard of living up, so that you can be My messenger to these people in a way they can understand and accept."

God wants to bring us to a place where we can be willing and obedient on a full stomach, as well as on an empty one. Paul learned this lesson and passes it on to us in Philippians 4:12, 13:

> I know how to live on almost nothing or with everything. I have learned the secret of contentment in every situation, whether it be a full stomach or hunger, plenty or want; for I can do everything God asks me to do with the help of Christ who gives me strength and power.

Most of us know more about being dependent on God when we have nothing than when we have a great deal. We have more experience dwelling in the wilderness than tasting of the good of the promised land. While the wilderness is a necessary experience in our Christian lives, *we were never meant to be permanent residents there*. We must go through the wilderness because we need to learn dependence on God. When we learn genuine dependence on Him, and when we stop forgetting Him as soon as things run smoothly for a while, we don't need the reminders of the wilderness any longer. We then have an open invitation to enter the land God has waiting for us.

We may receive the fullness of His promise in one area of our lives and go through a wilderness experience in another area. There is a vast difference between genuine wilderness *experience* and a wilderness *complex*. Judy and I went through a wilderness experience in the area of finances while I was in Bible college.

When I first began to trust that God would supply my financial needs, I prayed, "Lord, I depend on You for my finances." Almost immediately the Lord began supplying financial help from people who sent it through the mail. I thought, "Thank You, Lord. You are providing in a wonderful way." Then came a period of two months when, although I looked expectantly into my mailbox every day, it was always empty! I became very upset and wondered what was the matter with God. Finally I realized that I had shifted my dependency from God to the mailbox. God knew my heart and stopped the money through the mail so that I could get back my perspective and realize who was the *real* source of my supply. I learned that God can supply in any way He chooses, but He wants me not to become dependent on the *provision*—but on Him.

As we learn to depend on God for finances, finances are no problem, whether one is a millionaire or living happily on an income of fifty dollars a week. Dependency on God must be more than lip service!

God desires to bring us into the promised land in *every area* of our lives. This was His plan for the Israelites, and it is His plan for us. He wants to provide for us—keep us in health—out of debt—united and strong as families—and filled with joy, peace and love. He wants to bless us in order that others may see His goodness and, in turn, come to Him to be blessed.

God's original plan for the Israelites was that they might be an example to their day and world of His goodness and His ability to undertake in their behalf. They were chosen so that they might be instruments in His hands in drawing the entire world to Himself. Today we are His chosen people. God doesn't want us wandering around in the wilderness years on end. He wants to bless and undertake for us in order that we may be an example to our confused and needy world. He wants our lives, homes, children to reflect His glory so that those who do not know Him will be drawn to Him.

When people come to us, as individuals, or to our church

doors, God doesn't want them to turn sadly away because our lives are shallow and empty—no different from the lives they seek so desperately to escape. He wants Christians to be noticeably different—not because they *talk* Christianity, but because our lives are radiant with a joy and power which only Christ can give. If our lives—at church—home—in the neighborhood—at work—were like that, then the tired, sick, desperate, the rebels, and doubters would all come to us seeking—and finding answers.

Jeremiah wrote about this deep desire on God's part:

And I will cleanse away all their sins against me, and pardon them. Then this city will be an honor to me, and it will give me joy and be a source of praise and glory to me before all the nations of the earth! The people of the world will see the good I do for my people and will tremble with awe!

Jeremiah 33:8, 9

Jesus expressed His Father's desire this way:

You are the world's light—a city on a hill, glowing in the night for all to see. Don't hide your light! Let it shine for all; let your good deeds glow for all to see, so that they will praise your heavenly Father.   Matthew 5:14–16

God wants to restore our lives and cleanse every bit of rebellion from our hearts. His desire is that our lives be a source of praise and glory to His goodness. When this is accomplished, we can move from the wilderness into the promised land and be the fulfillment of Jesus' commands to be a light in our world to God's glory.

Remember, we were never meant to be permanent wilderness-dwellers. We are to learn *how* to walk through the wilderness into His provision.

4

The Law of the Four *Ps*

Christianity is not complicated. The relationship between God and man can be understood in terms simple enough for a child to grasp. Yet, the spiritual implications of these truths bring the wisest of men to a point of awe.

Christianity in operation is not only practical but it is also completely dependable. In His dealings with men, God gives us a straightforward conditional statement: "If you will do this, I will do that; on the other hand, if you refuse, this will happen." In theology, this is called an objective propositional revelation. God gives us a proposition; if we follow it, the outcome will be just as He promised.

We have seen that God always makes a conditional promise, followed by a problem situation where temptation will provoke a decision either to fulfill God's condition or ignore it. The fulfillment of the promise (or the provision) cannot come until after we have made the decision—and then only if we decide to obey God's Word.

I have found this pattern to be absolutely invariable in God's workings with us. (*See* biblical examples in Appendix.) It is consistent throughout the Bible as well as in my personal experience. I have never found an exception to this rule. An easy way to remember the pattern is to think of it as *The Law of the Four Ps.*

God gives us *A Promise,* which is linked to *A Principle* (or condition), followed by *A Problem* (temptation in the wilderness)—leading to *A Provision!*

Understanding the workings of this law, we would then realize that unfilled promises should not be the normal Christian experience. *The promises are meant to be fulfilled.* Trouble is that most of us bog down in the problem because we don't understand it as part of God's pattern. I used to think that if I prayed to receive a promise and then stumbled into a problem, it meant my prayer was not going to be answered. Somehow I had received a problem *instead* of a provision. According to the Law of the Four *Ps,* the problem doesn't come *instead of*—but *as part of*—or *means of* obtaining the provision.

Many Christians find it difficult to understand how God would use a problem as part of His plan to bring us into provision. We want to blame the problem on the devil, and think he interfered and upset God's intention. There is no question but that the devil is in the picture—but he is only there with God's permission. We need the problem to prepare for God's provision. The Apostle James saw this principle and wrote: "Blessed is the man who shall endure temptation: for *when he is tried, he shall receive . . .*" (James 1:12 KJV).

The Bible contains innumerable cases where we can observe the Law of the Four *Ps* at work. They are put there to teach us to expect this same pattern in our own lives.

Once we claim a promise, we should make certain we understand the principle—that *how* to turn our promise into provision. Then we should expect some sort of situation where we will be tempted to ignore God's Word. If we decide to ignore His Word, there cannot be a provision. If we decide to fulfill the condition or the principle, we can confidently expect God to bring us into the provision.

The pitfall right here is that we are apt to be caught unaware when the problem arises. We seldom see the connection between it and the promise. Therefore, we are likely to become discouraged and fail. Expecting the problem keeps us prepared, and once we recognize the wilderness situation, we can usually go through it with less pain and in a shorter period of time.

The Old Testament Speaks

We shall use the wilderness journey of the Israelites as our prime test case. The writers of the New Testament used this same experience as a pattern for all believers because the *promises* God established for them are offered to us, as well, through the Person of Jesus Christ. The Israelites received their promise in Egypt when God said, "I will lead you to a wonderful land flowing with milk and honey." When we accepted Jesus Christ as our Saviour, we became eligible for the same promise: "I will lead you into a place of abundant blessings."

Our map shows us that God brought the children of Israel to Mount Sinai and gave them the *principles*—the Ten Commandments—and the *condition*—"If you are willing and obedient, you will eat of the good of the land." Then came the wilderness, or the *problem.*

And why did God provide this wilderness experience? For the same reason a temptation experience is necessary for us

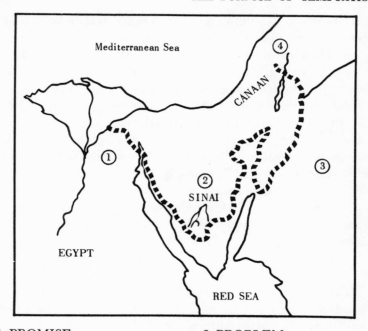

1 PROMISE   3 PROBLEM
  (Inheritance)   (Wilderness)

2 PRINCIPLE   4 PROVISION
  (Commandments)   (Land)

(See Appendix)

today. We need to learn who we are and who God is in a
way we will never forget. Thus, we can safely come into our
provision without becoming haughty, proud, and consequently destroy ourselves. Listen as Moses speaks for God:

> Do you remember how the Lord led you through the wilder-
> ness for all those forty years, humbling you and testing you
> to find out how you would respond, and whether or not you
> would really obey him? . . . For when you have become

full and prosperous and have built fine homes to live in, and
when your flocks and herds have become very large . . .
that is the time to watch out that you don't become proud
and forget the Lord your God who brought you out of your
slavery in the land of Egypt . . . He did it so that you would
never feel that it was your own power and might that made
you wealthy. Always remember that it is the Lord your God
who gives you power to become rich, and he does it to fulfill
his promise to your ancestors.   Deuteronomy 8:2, 12–18

The purpose of the wilderness is always to make us recognize our own insufficiency and God's all-sufficiency. Once
we realize this, willingness and obedience follows. When I
recognize that I cannot do something on my own, I should
be willing to give up trying to do it in my own strength and
be obedient to the command of God who *can* get it done.

Salvation

God's gift of salvation is subject to the Law of the Four
Ps, too. God *promises salvation* to those who believe in His
Son, Jesus Christ (John 3:16). The principle is our faith in
Him: "So now, since we have been made right in God's
sight by faith [principle] in his promises, we can have real
peace with him [provision] because of what Jesus Christ our
Lord has done for us" (Romans 5:1).

Somewhere between the promise, principle, and provision lies a wilderness area where we will be beset with
doubts and the temptation to disbelieve God's Word. Some
of us are prepared for doubts in this area. Evangelists and
evangelical organizations circulate booklets advising new
Christians to memorize God's promises of salvation. They
know these Scriptures will be needed to combat the doubts.
Salvation is based on: "God said it; I believe it; that settles
it in my heart." This is good advice. Feelings are dangerous

and false indicators of what is really true. We all know that we can be saved without *feeling* saved. So we learn to stand on God's Word, choosing to believe Him rather than our feelings. This is the essence of faith—believing what God has said, regardless of what our senses or the circumstances seem to indicate.

Today multitudes of Christians are struggling in their first wilderness of doubts about forgiveness of sins. They come to the altar again and again saying, "I just don't *know*. Maybe I better ask God to save me again." They have never fully understood the principle and they are totally unprepared for the problem. *There is no way to get to the provision of real peace in God except through the problem of doubt.* You must come to the point of *deciding*—in spite of some convincing factors of feelings and rational doubts—that God's Word is to be trusted. You must *choose* to believe that Christ is indeed God's Son who died for your personal rebellion and sins. You will never be convinced or have peace with God any other way. No overwhelming proof will come your way before you make your decision. The peace and assurance can only come after you have decided to trust God's Word in the midst of uncertainty. That is faith.

Acquaint yourself with God's Word on the matter, and then consider it as fact. Concerning salvation, God says this, in effect, in John 3:16: "He loves us enough to have given his son, Jesus Christ, so that whoever believes on him (clings to, trusts in, and relies on him) will not be lost but have life forever." God's part is already an established fact, done and sealed by Christ on the cross.

The condition left up to us is that we turn from our efforts at saving ourselves, admit our rebellion (sin), accept Christ as our Saviour as well as our Lord and Master. This makes us eligible for another promise: "Those who believe in Christ

will receive power to become the sons of God" (*see* John
1:12). If we do our part of the condition (cling to, rely on,
trust and believe in Jesus Christ), we can be absolutely
certain that God has done His. We have His Word on it.
But we can also be certain that our sense of security and
peace in God can only come after a period of serious doubt
and questioning.

Healing

Healing is another gift subject to the Law of the Four *Ps*.
A man once asked me, "If you can't get healed when you
ask for it, how do you know you are saved when you ask
for it?" I wrestled with this question for some time before
there was an adequate answer.

If we were taught the principle of healing as thoroughly
as we are taught the principle of salvation, we would be able
to hold on to our healing. I do not mean to imply that healing is as universal a promise as salvation. The Bible tells us
that *all* who call on the name of Jesus Christ shall be saved.
The same universal promise does not apply to healing, because illness, aging, and physical death are part of our world.
The Bible does not promise that our sick world will be completely healed before Christ returns.

However, God *does* promise to heal; and when that promise is given to an individual, the fulfillment is meant to be
received. In that case, I believe if the promise of healing
is accepted in the same way that we accept our promise of
salvation, we will be able to lay claim to the promise of
healing in spite of doubts, feelings, and recurring symptoms.

I am convinced that God intends for Christians to enjoy
greater health and a higher percentage of healings than we
see evidenced in our churches today. It is safer to expound
on Paul's "thorn in the flesh" (2 Corinthians 12:7), than to

risk teaching on healing. There is a serious discrepancy between what God has made available to us in Christ and what we are actually experiencing. In a large measure, this is due to the fact that most of us consider our feelings as the only reliable gauge for whether or not we are physically well. If healing follows the Law of the Four *Ps*, we should expect the problem to contain physical symptoms designed to test our faith in God's promise.

A woman was slowly dying of multiple sclerosis. She believed that God would heal her and many people had prayed for her. Still she continued to get worse. She kept on pleading with God and told her friends she thought He would answer her prayers soon. However, the time came when she was placed in a hospital, and she lost her eyesight and ability to move her limbs. The doctors feared she had only a day or two more to live.

One of her friends visited her and leaning over her bedside said, "Stop waiting for God to heal you soon. Accept the fact that He has healed you already. Thank Him for it and stop thinking about how sick you *feel*." It was as if a bright light had gone on in the dying woman's mind. She suddenly understood why she was feeling worse all the time. She had been keeping her mind on her feelings instead of on Christ's finished work. She began to thank God, and within hours, her body responded. In a few days, she was home from the hospital and back on her feet. When she tells her story, she remarks that if she had stayed in bed waiting for God to heal her instead of accepting that He had already done it, she would have been dead in spite of God's provision waiting for her.

The Israelites died in the wilderness in spite of God's provision of a Promised Land because they could never accept the problem as part of God's plan. Many who could be healed are not—because they do not understand how to go through the problem into the provision of health. In that particular wilderness, you will be faced with the choice to either believe God's Word that He has healed you, or your own sense and feelings that you are still sick.

The many healings recorded in the Bible are all different, but there is one common denominator throughout—*faith*. Faith, we know, is the determination to believe, trust in, and rely on God's Word over and above what our senses or circumstances may tell us. Faith alone can take us through the problem into the provision.

Fruit of the Spirit

The Bible tells us that the characteristics of a normal Christian life should be an abundance of love, joy, peace, patience, kindness, goodness, faithfulness, gentleness, and self-control. We only have to look into our own hearts to realize that this description seldom fits our daily experience. The reason for this is that these expected Christian qualities are provided for us in promise form, and can become translated into real experience only through the workings of the Law of the Four *Ps*. Galatians 5:22, 23 gives us the principle and the promise: "When the Holy Spirit controls our lives he will produce this kind of fruit in us: love, joy, peace, patience, kindness, goodness, faithfulness, gentleness and self-control . . . ."

Do you see the condition: that the Holy Spirit must control our lives? He must produce the fruit. They cannot be produced by willpower; they grow only when we are rightly connected to Christ through the Holy Spirit. Between the

promise, principle, and the provision, we expect a problem.
In this case, it is a wilderness situation where the fruit of
the Spirit will either be given an opportunity to grow—or be
crushed by our self-will.

In John 15:1–4, Jesus describes *how* fruit is encouraged to
grow:

> I am the true Vine and my Father is the Gardener. He lops
> off every branch that doesn't produce. And he prunes those
> branches that bear fruit for even larger crops. He has already
> tended you by pruning you back for greater strength and
> usefulness by means of the commands I gave you. Take care
> to live in me, and let me live in you. For a branch can't
> produce fruit when severed from the vine. Nor can you be
> fruitful apart from me.

The lopping off (the pruning back for greater strength
and greater production) is an apt description of a wilderness experience. Our real-life experience comes through circumstances in which we are squeezed to the point where
we can't continue to act loving and patient in our own
strength. We are forced to admit to our own unlovingness
and impatience. The temptation comes to provoke a decision.
We can either admit our insufficiency, confess our unlovingness, and turn ourselves over to God, asking Him to *make*
us loving—or we can refuse to see God's hand in the problem, explode, and blame the whole thing on the terrible
circumstances we have fallen into.

When we pray for God to make us more loving, we can
expect Him to put us into a problem situation where we are
confronted with people who are difficult to love—so difficult
that it is impossible for us to love them of ourselves. The
provision—a new ability to love people—comes only as we

go through the problem and allow Christ to take over and control our natural inclinations.

The fruit of the Spirit does not grow *automatically* in a Christian's life—only as one deliberately chooses to stick to God's principles through a problem situation.

Marriage

God gave wonderful promises concerning Christian marriage. When Jesus was asked about marriage, He answered: "Don't you read the Scriptures? . . . In them it is written that at the beginning God created man and woman, and that a man should leave his father and mother, and be forever united to his wife. The two shall become one—no longer two, but one! And no man may divorce what God has joined together" (Matthew 19:4–6).

The promise is that God intended to make two different people, with two different personalities, into one harmonious union. God promises to do it, because He knows two human beings cannot join themselves together in *perfect union* in their own strength. Most couples start out very much in love, but God intended to remake their human love into something far more reliable, enduring, exciting, and joyous than anything they could experience in their own strength.

Between that glorious promise and God's intended provision, must necessarily come a wilderness of problems. The difficulties of the wilderness are designed to show us that our own resources are insufficient to make a satisfying marriage union. God wants to make our marriage in such a way that we can never claim credit for it. We have to recognize that He made our marriage—and He alone can maintain it.

God wants us to realize that our marriage cannot succeed

simply because we feel we are so well suited to each other—
so kind and understanding—so much in love. He wants us to
know that our marriage can be gloriously happy only because God makes it possible. On our own, we would have
made a terrible mess. Our personalities would clash—our
interests differing—and we would be headed toward stormy
seas.

No marriage—regardless of how much the couple is in love
at the start—can come into the fullness of a really mature,
rich, and permanent relationship without going through
some difficult problems. Unfortunately, very few couples see
their problems as part of God's plan to bring them into this
fuller relationship. A majority remain in the wilderness—
enduring a family life that, at best, is only a shadow of the
joy God promised. A growing number of Christian couples
follow the custom of their non-Christian friends and neighbors—when things get too rough, they divorce. The marriage
perishes in the wilderness.

When the Pharisees asked Jesus why Moses had permitted
easy divorce, Jesus answered, "Moses did that in recognition
of your hard and evil hearts, but it was not what God had
originally intended" (Matthew 19:8). So we see it is not
God's original intent that any marriage end in divorce. If
we understand His promise, learn His conditions and principles, learn to hold on to them through the inevitable problems—then we will come into provision. When God has made
husband and wife *one* in joyous union, divorce will be an
impossible thought.

If you have already spent time in a wilderness situation
in your marriage, ask God to teach you the principles—hang
on to them through difficult circumstances, and you will soon
enter your promised land. Unfulfilled promises are not the

normal Christian life—neither are unhappy marriages. God wants to transform them into abundant provision.

Having realized the necessity for the *problem,* we are now prepared to take a closer look at this vital area and discover some possibilities for moving into the abundant provision God wants us to receive.

5

Alternatives in the Problem

The problem is the central part of our journey from promise to provision. Our behavior in the problem determines to what extent—how soon—or even, whether or not—we'll come into our provision!

Returning to our test case (the Israelites and their problems), and comparing them with our own experiences, we can observe three basic alternatives facing us during the problem or wilderness.

(1) ANOTHER LAP   Our initial negative response to the problem leads to an extended stay in the wilderness. God provides a similar set of circumstances to give us a chance at another lap through the same problem.

(2) BLEACHED BONES   Repeated negative responses cause us to perish in the wilderness. Our continuing hardened attitude eventually prevents us from coming into the provision.

(3) STAND AND ENTER   If our response is positive and

we choose to stand on God's principles through the problem, we are able to enter our provision with little delay.

As we examine each of these alternatives, remember the Law of the Four *Ps*—the possibility of falling prey to a wilderness complex—and the goodness and patience of our God.

Another Lap

When the Israelites entered their wilderness experience, they had just come across the Red Sea and had seen God take care of their enemies behind them. They had received their promise in Egypt and had learned the basic principle: *If* they would only trust God and obey Him, He would lead them safely through the wilderness ahead.

We know they believed in both promise and principle because we read in Exodus that the entire nation sang a song of victory and praise to God:

. . . I will sing to the Lord, for he has triumphed gloriously;
.   .   .   .
The Lord is my strength, my song, and my salvation.
He is my God, and I will praise him.
.   .   .   .
You have led the people you redeemed.
But in your lovingkindness
You have guided them wonderfully
To your holy land.
The nations heard what happened, and they trembled.
Fear has gripped the people of Philistia.
The leaders of Edom are appalled,
The mighty men of Moab tremble;
All the people of Canaan melt with fear.
Terror and dread have overcome them.

O Lord, because of your great power they won't attack us!
Your people whom you purchased
Will pass by them in safety.
You will bring them in and plant them on your mountain,
Your own homeland, Lord—
The sanctuary you made for them to live in.
Jehovah shall reign forever and forever.
   Then Miriam the prophetess, the sister of Aaron, took a
timbrel and led the women in dances.

                                        Exodus 15:1, 2, 13–18, 20

The Israelites were confident that God would take care
of them because they had just seen how He drowned an
entire army in the Red Sea. Had their first problem in the
wilderness been an army pursuing them across the desert,
I think they would have continued their singing, expecting
God to repeat His miracle.

I recognize myself in the Israelites. Many times I have
praised God for something He has done in my life, and then
turned around, expecting Him to do the same thing over
again. I seek to anticipate *how* God is going to solve a problem, or the nature of the problem, which causes me to fall
flat on my face when God moves in *His* way.

Immediately after the singing and dancing, God led the
former slaves into the wilderness of Shur where they were
three days without water. Then they arrived at Marah and
couldn't drink the water in the spring because it was bitter.
God demonstrated the condition of their hearts by sending
a problem different in kind from the one they had seen Him
solve before. Did they or didn't they trust Him to provide
for them?

They did not respond as He had hoped they would. They
didn't say, "God parted the Red Sea before us. Surely He
can turn bitter water into sweet water. We'll just praise Him

and watch Him perform another miracle." Instead, they turned to Moses and demanded, "Must we die of thirst here!" Because of their negative response, they extended their stay in the wilderness. God brought about another set of circumstances, providing them with another opportunity to choose to trust Him. They had to *take another lap.*

We often anticipate that God will work in one way and are unaware that He is already at work in our problem—where we least expect Him to be! If you have a difficult boss, you may pray that God will take care of your enemy. You expect God to either take that mean boss away or turn him into a nice guy. Instead your boss seems to be harder than ever. Isn't God answering your prayer? Of course, He is, but in a different way than you expected. God is dealing with the *real* enemy—your own pride and unyielding ego. And He is permitting the boss to become more difficult so that you will turn to Him and ask Him to take your pride

and unyielding spirit and make you yield to Him instead.
When you do, you may find that your boss has become sur-
prisingly kind and understanding overnight!

Identifying the root cause of our problem makes it easier
to accept. We almost always make the mistake of blaming
our difficulties on our circumstances—expecting God to
change them—when we should realize that our own attitude
is causing the problem. God can change our circumstances
instantly if He wants to. When He doesn't, it is because He
wants to change something in us. The circumstances are
there to bring about what needs to be changed.

The continuing story of the wilderness journey of the
people of Israel is told not only in the Book of Exodus, but
also in Leviticus, Numbers, and Deuteronomy. We pick up
with their experiences at Elim. Here they camped among
palm trees beside twelve springs of water. Once more God
showed them He could provide. Next they were led into the
Sin wilderness. Here they couldn't find anything to eat. We
recognize they were back facing the same problem in a
slightly different guise. Instead of bitter water, they now
had lack of food.

If our first response to a problem is negative, God will
meet our immediate demand and move us on, providing a
similar set of circumstances to confront us with the same
choice again—to trust Him and stand on His principles—or
to ignore His principles and complain. We may not even
recognize the pattern for a while, but there will be continuing difficulties of a similar nature—slowly increasing in
severity.

Now we find the Israelites complaining even more about
the lack of food than they had complained about the water.
Gone was the praise and confidence of their singing and
dancing. Gone was the assurance they had received when

God turned bitter water to sweet. But God was patient with His chosen people. That evening it rained quail and in the morning manna covered the desert. Again God had responded to their complaints, demonstrating His love and ability to provide.

The following lap around the mountain led to Rephidim, where there was no water at all. Here they were back facing a situation very similar to the one they had seen God solve before. How would they react? Would they remember His miracles and confidently expect another? No, it was more complaints—this time almost to the point of wanting to stone Moses. But God led them to Mount Horeb and instructed Moses to beat on a rock with his rod, and water gushed out. Moses named the place Massah, meaning, "tempting Jehovah to slay us"; for it was here the people of Israel argued against God and tempted Him to slay them by saying, "Is Jehovah going to take care of us or not?"

The wilderness between Egypt and Canaan can be crossed on foot in less than two weeks, but it took the Israelites forty years! With each lap, each confrontation with the problem, they chose to complain instead of trusting God. With each lap their bitterness grew and their rebellion hardened. They didn't wait when Moses went up on Mount Sinai, but built themselves a golden calf in direct disobedience to the command God had just given them. They murmured and complained all the way across the desert; and when they finally arrived at the border of the Promised Land and saw that it was full of fortified cities and enemies—some of them even giants—they panicked and refused to enter in.

Bleached Bones

Twelve spies went over the border to look at the land. Ten of them said the land couldn't be taken. The last two, Joshua

and Caleb, remembered God's words and believed them. They wanted to go into their provision, but the people refused to follow. Ten times the Israelites had tried God's patience—and finally the laps gave out. Their hearts were hardened in rebellion and God lost His patience with them.

Christianity is something more than repeated forgiveness every time we do wrong. It also has to do with willingness and obedience. If we harden our hearts in the wilderness, the second alternative will be our end; our *bones will bleach* —we will perish in the problem—we will never come into the fullness of provision. This does not mean a loss of salvation. God forgave the Israelites for their rebellion, but He refused to let them enter the Promised Land.

Moses pleaded with God to pardon the sins and God answered:

All right, I will pardon them as you have requested, but I vow by my own name that just as it is true that all the earth shall be filled with the glory of the Lord, so it is true that

not one of the men who has seen my glory and the miracles
I did both in Egypt and in the wilderness—and ten times
refused to trust and obey me—shall even see the land I promised to this people's ancestors. Numbers 14:20-23

God said He would forgive the people. They did not lose
their salvation, but they lost the opportunity to receive the
fulfillment of the promise. Their bones bleached in the wilderness. They perished spiritually, although they were actually in possession of the promise.

The bleached bones are a sad spectacle in the desert, but
it becomes our alternative if we continually respond nega-
tively to the problems confronting us on our many laps
around the wilderness. There are bleached bones strewn
across many a modern-day wilderness.

After continual resistance, there may come a point of no
return in God's dealings with us. Listen to this turning point
in our test case:

Then the ten spies who had incited the rebellion against
Jehovah by striking fear into the hearts of the people were
struck dead before the Lord. Of all the spies, only Joshua
and Caleb remained alive. What sorrow there was throughout the camp when Moses reported God's words to the
people!

They were up early the next morning and started towards
the Promised Land.

"Here we are!" they said. "We realize that we have sinned,
but now we are ready to go into the land the Lord has
promised us."

But Moses said, "It's too late. Now you are disobeying the
Lord's orders to return to the wilderness. Don't go ahead
with your plan or you will be crushed by your enemies, for
the Lord is not with you. Numbers 14:36-42

This is a fearful thought: that God will forgive us our sins against Him, but unless we allow Him to prepare us—unless we accept fully His principles and His problems—*He cannot bring us into the promised land.* How tragic that Christians who know His promises may spend their lives wandering in the wilderness—unable to ever see those promises turned into provision. *In the end—bleached bones!*

Stand and Enter!

The third alternative, *stand and enter,* was open to only two of the Israelites of that first generation—Caleb and Joshua. As spies in the Promised Land, they had seen the fortified cities and the armed giants with their own eyes. But they had remembered God's promise and were confident that He would deliver the land into their hands. Forty years

PROMISED LAND

later, Joshua and Caleb led the new generation across the River Jordan into the Promised Land!

If we fail on our first lap around, there will be another opportunity to face the same principle. We will get another choice between standing on God's Word or refusing to obey Him. Often we do not even recognize a situation as God's confrontation with a problem until we have failed it once or twice. Here is one such experience.

A woman had heard me talk about the Law of the Four *Ps* and the three alternatives in facing the problem. She recognized that for years she had been taking laps around a problem which had crystallized into resentment towards her mother. Upon returning home, she prayed that God would help her forgive her mother and love her. She fully expected something to happen to bring about a change in her feelings.

Something did happen—the situation took a drastic turn for the worse. She discovered that her mother had hidden some correspondence from her. The hurt was so deep that she exploded in a fit of anger, accusing her mother of trying to manipulate her life. Later that evening, she realized that God had brought her into the difficult situation to provide her with an opportunity to forgive her mother. Having failed in the problem, she knew that she could expect another lap. She decided to be on her guard for another confrontation with her mother.

A week went by and she didn't see her mother. But one evening, her husband told her that their daughter, who was away at college, had failed a class and he had permitted her to transfer to another course. While her husband was still speaking, the old familiar resentment began to rise within her: "They always do things behind my back . . . my husband and daughter and my mother. . . ." Suddenly she saw the pattern of her own thoughts! This was the other lap she had been expecting. For the first time she realized that the problem wasn't resentment towards her mother—that was just a symptom. The problem was her own pride which often manifested itself in a strong tendency to be in charge of every situation and manipulate others according to her own will.

Silently she prayed, "God, forgive me. Thank You for showing me the way I really am. Take my prideful ego and as I yield myself to You, make me the mother, wife, and daughter You want me to be."

Her husband looked at her with concern and continued, "Susy and I didn't want to worry you. We knew how much you wanted Susy to be a lawyer. But she really is much happier with the prospect of becoming a veterinarian. You know she has always loved to care for sick animals." The crisis point had passed, and the mother was able to smile and honestly say that she was happy Susy was doing what she had always wanted to do.

A few days later when this woman went to see her mother, she discovered that the old resentment had melted away. She was able to understand that her mother had hidden those letters in order to save her from hurt. She could ask forgiveness for the angry remarks she had made the last time they were together. For the first time in many years she felt genuine love for her mother.

After many years in the wilderness—with repeated laps around the same problem—she had at last been able to recognize God's way of presenting her with the choice of trusting His principles or continuing in her own stubborn way, resulting in a final perishing in the wilderness. By standing on God's principle (that is, yielding her pride and asking forgiveness and help), she was able to enter her promised land

—a warm and genuine relationship, not only with her mother, but also with her husband and daughter. For years, they had suffered under her continual compulsion to control and manipulate.

God is patient and permits us another lap. This continues until we have succeeded in the problem or become so hardened that another lap will make no difference whatsoever. The laps become gradually more severe—or obvious—in order to bring a recognition of wrong reaction. God doesn't want to press us into a severe problem. If we understand the principle and succeed in rejecting the temptation to disobey the first time around, we are ready to move right into the provision without delay. He longs to show us that a difficult situation is always a doorway to the promised land—if we are willing to meet His conditions.

Once I went to the house of a potter in Peru and watched him carefully form and shape clay vessels. Then he put them in a hot oven to bake. After a certain length of time he opened the oven door and I felt the blast of the heat against my face. The potter pulled out one of the vessels, flicked the rim, and I could hear it go *clunk*. He returned the pot to the oven and I asked him, "How do you know when it is done?" Smilingly, he replied, "When it sings! When I flick the rim and it gives out a beautiful resonant note, then I know it is ready."

God permits us to stay in the heat of the problem, lap after lap, until we have learned to sing. Then we are ready to move into our provision. We have become vessels prepared to be filled with the abundant love, joy, and peace He has promised.

6

The Religious Question

How we come through the problem—or wilderness—depends on our response to temptation. We have mentioned that temptation means putting to the proof—whether for good or evil. What is being put to the proof is our willingness to be totally yielded, or obedient, to God's Word. Temptation doesn't become real until God has given us His Word and established His principle in our understanding.

For example, I say to my son: "Don't use your sister's bike! If you do, I'll have to punish you." I make certain my son understands. "Yes, Dad, I heard you. I won't use my sister's bike." Then comes the day when he is at home alone—the garage door is open—and there is his sister's new bicycle. What happens next? My son will be confronted with the question: "Did Dad *really* say not to take my sister's bike? And, if he did, did he *really* mean that he would punish me if I disobey?"

When we are in the midst of temptation, *God's principle will always be questioned*. This is the essence of temptation! We shall refer to this critical point in our journey through the wilderness as *the religious question*. This question may take any number of forms, but it always amounts to a doubting of God's Word or His intentions: "Hath God said . . . ?" It always seeks to dishonor God.

Temptation came to Eve in the form of the religious question. The serpent said to her, "Really? *None* of the fruit of the garden? God says you mustn't eat *any* of it?" (Genesis 3:1). The first question was designed to test Eve to see if she remembered what God *had* said. She replied, "Of course we may eat it. It's only the fruit from the tree at the *center* of the garden that we are not to eat. God says we must not eat it—or even touch it or we will die" (vs. 2, 3).

If we *know* God's words, the religious question will then throw doubt on the *validity* of His words or intentions to do as He said. Notice the serpent's next approach: ". . . You'll not die! God knows very well that as soon as you eat it, you will become like him—for your eyes will be opened—you will be able to distinguish good from evil" (v. 4).

Here the serpent is questioning the character of God. He is implying, "He's a mean old God. He just doesn't want you to be as smart as He is—or to enjoy life as much!"

Note the similarity in Satan's approach to the boy in our opening example: "That mean old Dad, he just won't let you have any fun. Just go ahead and take your sister's bike. Chances are he won't find out about it; and if he does, he's not really going to punish you like he said. You can always get out of it."

The religious question always strikes at the heart of the matter and forces us to make a decision. Shall I believe God's Word and obey Him—or shall I ignore Him and follow my own inclinations? God always arranges circumstances in such a way that the religious question will face us, because until it *has* been faced, there is always the possibility of double-mindedness, self-will, ego, or weakness hiding in our hearts— ready to trip us up at a critical moment.

The religious question must be faced and answered by all of us—and in all major areas of our lives. In effect, God says in His Word: "If you do these things that I command you, you will live and eat the good of the land . . . don't steal, don't lie, don't commit adultery, don't covet, don't have other gods before me, don't kill, honor your parents . . ." Then He sums it up with these words, "Love the Lord with all your heart and mind and might and love your neighbor as yourself" (*see* Matthew 23:38).

Did God *really* say that? All of us have been faced with this question, as well as the suggestion, "Those rules were made by a mean old God who doesn't want us to have any fun." Almost every young couple in love faces the religious

question, "Did God *really* say we shouldn't have sexual inter-
course before we're married? But we really love each other
and we're going to get married someday. What harm can it
possibly do?"

The religious question will always suggest that your own
way is the easier and better way (while God's way is difficult,
hard, and could not possibly lead to the fulfillment of your
dreams and ambitions). While you are in the grip of temptation, the religious question will present itself in the form of
deception, rationalization, and excuses—and you will find
that your reason and your senses are likely to be in direct
opposition to God's Word.

I once counseled a single woman who was torn with desire
for a man who was already married. His marriage wasn't a
happy one and from their first meeting they struck up a
friendship based on common interests—including a common
faith in God. Both were what I would call sincere Christians
who wanted to obey God's will. Their story followed a classic
pattern. They soon discovered that their friendship had
grown into "spiritual love." Later their affections grew
stronger and they found themselves on the verge of open
adultery. At this point the woman came to me for advice.

"Couldn't it be possible that God led us together?" she
asked hopefully. "Couldn't it be God's will? Our relationship
is so beautiful—it seems so right—and we feel so close to God
when we're together."

"What has God said about adultery?" I countered.

"We know that," she admitted, "but this is different. We
would get married if only his wife would give him a divorce."

"What are you going to do about God's commandment?"
I repeated.

She looked down and murmured, "I don't feel we are doing

anything wrong. How can God be opposed to something so real and beautiful?"

My next question was, "If you don't think God is serious about adultery, how do you know what He *is* serious about? Are you going to judge by your feelings or by what God has said?"

There were tears in her eyes as she acknowledged, "I understand what you mean. I'll have to go home and pray about it some more."

Three days later she was back, looking drawn and pale. "You know," she began, "I've so wanted this thing to be real —I've never wanted anything more in my life. But when I went home from your office, I read God's commandments and saw that what we were doing was against His Word. God calls it *sin*. It was an awful label to put on something I felt was the most wonderful thing that had ever happened to me." She bit her lip and was silent for a moment. "For several agonizing hours I wasn't so sure I wanted to turn away from it even though I *knew* it was wrong. I was afraid I'd never know real happiness away from him—and I was almost willing to turn my back on God for that. Never had temptation looked sweeter. Then I decided that deep down in my heart I wanted God's will more than anything else— even if it meant I would never know the love of a man."

For two days and nights following her decision, she said she had battled with constant waves of longing. "There were times when I walked the floor and said over and over again, 'Jesus, Jesus, I love You, Jesus.' I couldn't even read my Bible because my thoughts would stray."

(Temptation isn't real unless it involves the actual possibility of failure—a moment where you face the issue squarely and it is almost a toss-up which way you will take. Temptation looks so sweet—so sensible—so logical—you are on the verge of trading what it offers for what God has said. When you have faced that kind of decision, you have moved from lip service to God to wholehearted willingness to obey Him regardless of what it may cost you.)

Our interviews concluded with this statement: "On the third day the battle lessened in severity. It still hurts, but I feel like I've come out of prison. I can breathe again and I have a solid feeling inside that God's Word is more real than anything else in this world. I feel *safer* now than I have ever felt before, I *know* God will do what He has said."

Less than a year later, the young woman was married to another Christian. She told me, "God's promised land is ever so much better than the things you give up to follow His command." Temptation will always suggest an alternate route to the promised land—and, of course, the alternate road dead ends in the wilderness.

The religious question will also suggest a clever twisting of God's instructions. Therefore, it is essential that we clearly understand what God says in the first place. It should be elementary for a Christian to familiarize himself with God's Word. It is our guidebook on our journey through the wilderness to the promised land. If we follow the Law of the Four *Ps,* we need the Bible to check us at every point along the way.

First, check the promise. Is it according to God's Word? Don't take a promise out of context or accept a personal promise which you assume is from God without checking it against the character and principles of the Bible. You may have a strong desire for something and ask God for it with intensity. In prayer, or through circumstances, you may feel that God is telling you that He will grant your prayer. Always check your desire against what the Bible has to say. If it is inconsistent with either God's character or Word, then the promise is a false one.

A woman once prayed for the Lord to give her a beautiful antique dresser that had been standing in a neighbor's garage—thinking the neighbor did not really want it. After much petitioning, the woman thought God impressed on her that He would give her the dresser. After weeks of waiting, she thought God wanted her to go and claim it from the neighbor. As you can imagine, the result was a very unpleasant episode! The dresser was a family heirloom and the owner had planned to refinish it. Argument—hard feelings—disappointment followed.

If the woman who prayed for the dresser had understood God's principles, she would have recognized that He commands us *not to covet* what belongs to anyone else. She had coveted, and let herself be led astray by her own strong desires—prompted by the tempter who had suggested that God had said something in direct contradiction to His own commandments.

Beware of standing on the wrong promises. God will not promise you anything in contradiction to His own Word. Don't covet your neighbor's new car—his house—his dog—or his wife! And don't ever let yourself be deceived into believing that God promises to give you anything that rightfully belongs to someone else. Those are the kind of suggestions the religious question will put to us.

If your debts amount to $697.66, and you pray for God to provide what you need to pay them off—you may discover a billfold on the bus seat beside you. Inside it is exactly seven hundred dollars! Next comes the religious question like a flood.

"Did God *really* say you shouldn't steal?"

"Yes, that's one of the Ten Commandments, and it's in the New Testament, too."

"But don't you realize that God provided that billfold for you? It's exactly the amount you're praying for. Nobody will ever know you took it, just slip it out and leave the billfold in the seat."

God never contradicts Himself or goes against His own Word. Study the Bible, learn its principles, and be ready to face the religious question in all of its persuasive power.

Remember the questions we said were apt to come following your salvation? "Are you sure you are saved?"

"I think I am."

"But you don't feel saved and you don't act saved."

"But I believe in Jesus Christ and God's Word says I am saved."

Stand on God's Word against your feelings, emotions, and rationalizations.

A mother receives the promise that God will save her son. She goes home rejoicing—and the next time she sees him he is high on dope. Now comes the religious question.

"Did God *really* say He was going to save your son?"

"Yes, I'm sure."

"But look at him now. Do you think God can save him? Look at his miserable condition. God will never be able to reach him!"

Can you stand on God's Word, keep your eyes on *Him* instead of what your senses or reason tell you? God has saved dope addicts before. He'll do it again.

God says, "I will save your husband and make your home into a haven of Christian love and unity." There is your promise. Now comes the condition—the principle: "*If* you will trust Me and do your part as a Christian, submitting to your husband just as he is." "But, Lord . . . ."

That evening your husband gets drunk, curses your "silly religion," and leaves the house in anger. Up comes the religious question.

"Did God *really* say He was going to save your husband?"

"Yes."

"He'll never be able to change *him!*"

Can you stand on the promise, or do you give in to the temptation and have yourself a good cry?

"God can't do it—he is just too stubborn." That reaction will earn you another lap through the problem!

When God says He'll take you to a promised land, you can only get there if you follow His instructions. The religious question will always suggest alternate methods.

We are now going to take the story of God's dealings with Abraham in regard to fulfilling His promise that even though Abraham was an old man, he would have a son and that his descendants would be like the stars—too many to count! This is recorded in Genesis chapters 15 through 21.

Abram believed God's promise and went home and told his wife, Sarai. Since they both were old, they were certain they could have no children and reasoned that if God's promise was to become reality, Abram would have to sleep with another woman who could bear him a son. "Since the Lord has given me no children," Sarai said, "you may sleep with my servant girl, and her children shall be mine" (Genesis 16:3).

God had *not* instructed Abram to sleep with Sarai's servant girl. Abram and Sarai followed their own logic and reasoning, prompted by the religious question: "If God said you were to have many children, you better find a young woman who can bear them."

Since they did not follow God's instructions by waiting for God to give them a son, they found themselves on another lap through a problem made more severe by their wrong decision. Hagar, the servant girl, became pregnant and bore a son, Ishmael. But ill feeling had entered the household between Sarai and Hagar—and later Ishmael's descendants caused troubles for Israel.

Thirteen years after Ishmael's birth, God came to Abram again and told him He would make an everlasting covenant with him and his descendants. God said Abram would be the father of many nations and changed his name to Abraham—father of many nations. God also said, "Regarding Sarai, your wife, her name is no longer 'Sarai,' but 'Sarah' ('Princess'). And I will bless her and give you a son from her!" (17:15).

Abraham threw himself down on the ground to worship the Lord, but he laughed to himself, because he was one hundred years old, and Sarah was ninety. How could they possibly have a child? Abraham thought he must have heard wrong, and so he said to God, "Yes, do bless Ishmael" (v. 18).

"No," God replied, "that isn't what I said. Sarah shall bear you a son; and you are to name him Isaac ('Laughter') and I will sign my covenant with him forever, and with his descendants" (v. 19).

God was very specific and this time Abraham didn't try any shortcuts of his own—no more religious questions! He believed God, and after a year Sarah bore him a son and they named him Isaac. God intended to put Abraham to the test before He could fulfill His promise to make Isaac the father of many nations.

Later on God again tested Abraham's faith and obedience. This is recorded for us in chapter 22. Listen to God's instructions: "Take with you your only son—yes, Isaac whom you love so much—and go to the land of Moriah and sacrifice him there as a burnt offering upon one of the mountains which I'll point out to you" (vs. 1, 2).

The next morning Abraham got up early, chopped wood for a fire upon the altar, saddled his donkey, and took with him his son Isaac. Now can you imagine the barrage of religious questions swirling through this father's mind? "Did God *really* say to sacrifice Isaac? What about the covenant He made with Isaac? He promised to make him the father of many nations and said His covenant would be with him forever and with his descendants. If God is going to keep His covenant with Isaac, you better not sacrifice him."

"I must obey God's Word."

"You're being a fool, Abraham. You're going to destroy your covenant with God. If Isaac is killed there is no one left for God to use. God doesn't really mean for you to do it —it doesn't make sense. Besides, Isaac is everything you have in life—your only son—what do you think his mother will say?"

These questions cut to the core of Abraham's heart. This was the area where he was the most vulnerable. Isaac, his only son, meant more to him than anything else on earth. God had to bring Abraham to the test to see if Isaac meant more to him than obedience to God Himself. If there was any doublemindedness in Abraham, it would show itself now. And if there was any doublemindedness, God could not permit Abraham to receive the fulfillment of His great promise.

But Abraham stood firm and moved ahead to prepare for the sacrifice. Just as he lifted the knife, the Angel of God called to him saying, "Lay down the knife, don't hurt the lad in any way . . . for I know that God is first in your life— you have not withheld even your beloved son from me" (v. 12). Then Abraham noticed a ram caught by its horns in a bush. He sacrificed it instead of his son and named the place "Jehovah provides"—and it still goes by that name to this day. Abraham proved God could provide! He faced temptation and the religious questions, choosing to obey God's Word.

Do you see how these dealings with Abraham followed the Law of the Four *Ps?* He received the promise, followed by the principle, "Obey Me and trust Me." Then came the problem, and it looked as if the entire promise was being taken away. But Abraham stood on the principle and came through into the fulfillment of his provision.

Obedience alone will take you through to God's provision. But the religious question will have to be faced and answered. Be sure of what God wants you to do. Understand the principle, and be prepared to hold onto it, no matter how convincing the religious question may be!

7

Temptation in Delicate Balance

There's an old story about a man walking down the street and seeing the devil on the curbstone crying bitterly. "What's the matter?" questioned the bystander. To which the devil answered, "I'm always getting blamed for things I didn't get a chance to do!" The devil has long been our favorite scapegoat. When we do something we shouldn't, we say, "I didn't mean to, but the devil tempted me."

In reality, temptation hangs in a delicate balance between three participants: God, man, and the devil.

Yes, the devil is very much involved. Call him what you will—Satan, Lucifer, Old Clovefoot, or the Evil One! He is nevertheless a power to be reckoned with, and in the last ten years we have seen an increased recognition of his power in such phenomena as Satan worship, spiritism, witchcraft, and other eruptions of the occult. But powerful as Satan may be, he is *not* the prime mover in temptation. God is.

God ordained the workings of the Law of the Four *Ps*.

Let's go over it again. *He gave the promise and the principle and placed the problem as a preparation for receiving the provision.* Central to the problem is temptation with the religious questions bombarding us. This presents us with the choice of obeying or disobeying God's Word.

Now comes the question: Does God tempt a man? Many people quote James 1:13 to prove that God doesn't tempt a man: "And remember, when someone wants to do wrong, it is never God who is tempting him, for God never wants to do wrong and never tempts anyone else to do it." Yet we have just discussed how God tempted Abraham. Is there a contradiction here? No, there is no contradiction, for if we read the quotation from James carefully, we will note that he says that God *never tempts a man to do wrong.*

Here is the key! Temptation, we know, means to put to the proof *for good* or for malicious purposes. God never tempts a man for malicious purposes, but He *does* tempt a man— puts him to the proof—for *good* purposes. God puts us to the test in order to prepare us to receive the good things He has promised us.

How, in practical experience, does God tempt a man? For an answer, we take 2 Chronicles 32:31: ". . . God left him [Hezekiah] to himself in order to test [tempt] him and to see what he was really like."

This may raise another question. The Bible says God *left* Hezekiah. How can this be consistent with the many passages stating that God will never leave us or forsake us? Psalm 139 tells us: "If I go up to heaven, you are there; if I go down to the place of the dead, you are there. If I ride the morning winds to the farthest oceans, even there your hand will guide me . . ." (vs. 8–10).

Yet we are told that God *left* Hezekiah to test him and see what he was really like. We must come to see the difference between God's omnipresence and our conscious presence of Him. God left Hezekiah only in the sense that *He removed Hezekiah's awareness of His presence.* God was still there, but Hezekiah couldn't *feel* Him. It is when Daddy is gone that the real test of obedience comes to the children.

"Now, kids, when I'm gone, don't fight and don't get into the cookie jar!"

"Sure, Dad, we'll be good!"

Four hours later Daddy comes home and all but one cookie is gone!

How else can God find out what is in us? If we *feel* Him there all the time and we have that wonderful assurance of His presence, we won't be tempted to distrust Him in the problem.

First, God gives us His promise. Next, He teaches us the principle. Then, He withdraws our awareness of His presence and we enter the problem. Now we are faced with temptation and the religious question.

"Are you *sure* God cares about you?"

"Well, I think He does."

"But you don't *feel* Him around anymore, do you?"

"No . . . but . . . ."

"See! God doesn't care. He left you to yourself in the middle of this terrible situation!"

Here is temptation in delicate balance. When God withdraws our consciousness of *His* presence, He permits Satan to come near.

You may be certain Satan knows how to put the religious question—baiting the weaknesses that may be in us. Following our earlier quote from James 1:13, notice what verse 14 says: "Temptation is the pull of man's own evil thoughts and wishes."

Does this clear up some questions?

If Eve had *felt* God's presence in the garden, there wouldn't have been any problem. She would have walked up to the tree and God would have said, "Now Eve, remember—that's the tree I told you not to eat from. Be careful for that beautiful creature with the smooth voice is the devil trying to make you disobey Me and get you into trouble."

No, it doesn't work that way. God's purpose in withdrawing our consciousness of His presence is to make us face temptation and the religious question on the basis of His principle alone!

If the Israelites had *felt* the power of God's presence when

Moses left them to go up on Mount Sinai, they would never have been faced with the temptation to make an image of a golden calf. God would have been there, assuring them: "Here I am, My children. Don't worry, I'll always be with you—you will always be able to *feel* Me near you."

If God is to reveal to us what is really in our hearts, He *must* withdraw from us the sense-experience of His presence. Satan is then permitted to go to work with the religious question—and we are in the middle. The balance depends on us. We are forced to choose between Satan's suggestions and God's instructions. If there are evil desires in our hearts, we will respond to Satan's suggestions. Satan cannot succeed in drawing us away from God's instructions unless there is already a measure of double-mindedness in us—if there is nothing *inside,* there is nothing to which Satan can appeal.

Jesus made a statement in John 14:30 which clarifies this principle: "[Satan] is coming. And he has no claim on Me— he has nothing in common with Me—there is nothing in Me that belongs to him—he has no power over Me" (AMPLIFIED).

Satan only succeeds in tempting us in areas where we have something in common with him. That is where he has legal claim and can exert power. God wants to bring any such areas to the surface in order to cleanse them and fill us with His love. Temptation serves that purpose. These experiences we are going to share may not fit you, but if each of us will be honest, we can place ourselves in a similar situation. God knows how to suit the situation to the individual—and He will!

When God gets ready to work with us in a certain area, He withdraws our consciousness of His presence. Then Satan comes in and says, "God is gone now."

Feeling lonely and depressed, we agree, "Yes, He is gone now."

Satan reminds us, "Remember how you felt a few weeks ago? His presence made you feel warm and excited and challenged?"

"Yes, that's right," we respond miserably.

The tempter continues, "God has forsaken you. What you need is a good stiff drink to cheer you up!"

"But, God doesn't want me to drink."

The religious questions continue: "Doesn't He? He knows how weak you are and that you *need* a drink. He won't care if you have just one. It will make you feel a lot better. Go ahead . . . ."

So we succumb to the temptation to go to the bar—and have just one—and then another—and another. The next morning we feel even more miserable and mad at the devil. "He *made* me do it!"

Oh, no, he didn't! He only brought out what was already in our hearts. If no leanings in that direction had been inside, Satan could have had no appeal in that area. We need to understand this principle.

Let's look at another weakness. God says, "Christian, don't commit adultery."

"Yes, Lord. I understand that." Then God withdraws the consciousness of His presence and the temptation presents itself.

"Christian, you know your wife doesn't *really* understand you."

"That's right. She wasn't very nice at breakfast this morning."

Now that the door is open, Satan continues. "She doesn't really care about how hard you work or what a wonderful Christian you are—why don't you have a nice long talk with that pretty secretary of yours? *She* understands what a good job you are doing and what you go through."

God desires to give every Christian a solid marriage, and He wants to use us to help others who have problems with sex and marriage. What do you think God has to bring each of us through in order to prepare us for this provision?

Spiritual leaders aren't immune to temptation. In fact, they are prime targets because God wants to bring us over into the promised land so that we can show others the way through the problem. And there are no short-cuts between promise/principle/problem/provision for people who are "God's special servants." He must go through the problem to get into the provision—and in the problem he is faced with the temptation and the religious question. If there is something in him that needs to surface, it will show itself.

When I first understood that God was calling me to the ministry of pastor and teacher, I went through a wonderful period of joy in His presence. I thought, "This is wonderful. I am going to serve God and He will be right next to me for the rest of my life." Then I lost the *feeling* of God's presence and plunged into a time of conflict, fears, and doubts.

The religious question pounded me, "Do you mean God called *you* to the ministry? That's ridiculous! You know you don't have what it takes. You're even scared of facing people from the pulpit—God will never be able to use *you*." For months the conflict went on. From a rational point of view, the religious questions all made sense. I wasn't the studious type. I had been a rough-mouthed sailor when God touched me. How could *I* ever tell anybody about God and His Kingdom?

In Jeremiah 1:4–8, I found recorded a conversation between God and Jeremiah which meant much to me:

> The Lord said to me, "I knew you before you were formed within your mother's womb; before you were born I sanctified you and appointed you as my spokesman to the world."

"O Lord God," I said, "I can't do that! I'm far too young! I'm only a youth!"

"Don't say that," he replied, "for you will go wherever I send you and speak whatever I tell you to. And don't be afraid of the people for I, the Lord, will be with you and see you through."

Then he touched my mouth and said, "See, I have put my words in your mouth!"

But the religious question came back at me, "That was for Jeremiah! Why don't you forget the crazy idea and do something sensible for a living." The battle went on until one day I walked into the pulpit where I was to preach as a student minister, stood there facing the congregation half-scared, and said very firmly under my breath, "God has called me to preach. I *know* I'm not good enough, but *He's* going to make me able and *I won't turn back!*" Immediately the conflicting thoughts calmed down. I opened my mouth and began to speak—without any sensation of God's presence—but with a new determination that God's Word was all I needed to stand on.

Most of us use our feelings to measure our so-called spirituality. We say, "I feel spiritual today. I can just *feel* God's presence. It gives me goosebumps! Wasn't that a wonderful meeting last night? Couldn't you *feel* the Holy Spirit?" Then when the sensations and feelings are absent, we get down in the dumps and are prone to respond with, "I feel so depressed—I must not be very spiritual today. Perhaps I had better pray more—or go to another meeting tonight. God will be there."

We tend to be like the young man who went through the wedding ceremony and later on the sidewalk outside the church, he turned to his brand-new wife and said, "Honey,

I don't *feel* married, do you?" To which she replied, "Dear, you'd better adjust your feelings to fit the facts!"

While we are in the problem we will not be able to sense God's presence. God wants to free us from a dependency on our feelings in order that we can learn to stand on His Word alone. The following might be an actual explanation from God as to His workings in this "delicate balance" we are discussing:

> I'll be with you here in the wilderness. I give you My promise and I will explain My working principle. I will make sure that you understand. But when you get into the problem, I must remove your awareness of My presence. I'll be with you, but you will not be aware of it. It will *seem* as if you are all alone, facing the temptation and the religious question. It is necessary that I do this that you might see what I see in your heart. I promise you that over in the promised land you will feel My presence again.

When God allows us to sense His presence, it is on either side of the problem. In fact, the absence of a sensation of God's presence is one of the characteristics of the time in the problem. If we panic in the problem, as the Israelites did—time after time—and cry out for God to come and help us, He will; but the result will be another lap around the mountain and an extended stay in the wilderness.

A friend of mine had an amazing experience while he was in Bible college. One night he was alone in his room praying when the presence of God filled the room in a remarkable way. My friend was both excited and grateful. He could sense God saying, "I will never leave you or forsake you." It was a wonderful promise.

Then God withdrew the manifestation of His presence—

for two whole years. Never once during that time did my friend feel the least awareness of God's presence. But he repeated to himself, and to us: "God has told me He will never leave me or forsake me. I don't *feel* Him, but praise His Name. He is with me because He said so." After two years God's presence came again—more real than ever before. He felt called as a missionary to the Amazon Indians and is now deep in the jungles of Peru—alone. But he has learned to walk on the naked word of God.

When God withdraws His presence, Satan is allowed to come near with the religious question. *You are the one who stands in the delicate balance of temptation, and the outcome depends on your decision.* The religious question will always appeal to what is in your heart, and it can be a frightening experience to recognize what is hiding down there.

There is in every one of us a curiosity about evil. After God withdrew the consciousness of His presence from Eve, Satan came with his religious question, "Wouldn't you like to be wise and know good from evil?" Deep in Eve's heart was curiosity which raised the responding question, "I wonder what evil is like?" She made the decision between obeying God and listening to Satan's suggestion. It was the curiosity in her own heart that tipped the balance.

Young people are told not to do something and a battle ensues. "I wonder what it is like . . . I don't want to become a drug addict or a drunk . . . but I'd like to taste the drug or the drink just once!" A father once took his teen-aged boy into his library and told him all the books were his to read—except one volume up in the corner—telling him he was not mature enough to read it yet. After the father left the room, you know just which book the son reached for! Right! He said later, "If Dad had not mentioned that book, I would never have looked at it. It looked terribly dull and thick on the outside. But when I knew it was forbidden, the curiosity burned in me until I had a chance to look into it."

As long as curiosity eats away at us, we're vulnerable to temptation. It isn't easy for a young man or woman to turn away from temptation just because God or parents say they must not do something. It isn't easy to say no to experimenting with sex, without trying a little to see what it is like. Can you turn away from the book and magazine rack in the bus station or airport or supermarket without taking a quick little look? Satan comes with the clever suggestion that you ought to at least "be enlightened and *know* what the public is exposed to in this day and age."

The desire to *know* good from evil got the better of Eve. God wants us to be where we trust *His* judgment and take *His* word for what is good and evil. We don't need to be familiar with evil in order to choose good. Familiarity with evil is dangerous, even when it goes by the label of *enlightened understanding*. Paul tells us, "Don't even *think* about such things" (*see* Ephesians 5:12). Until we decide to put away our curiosity and obey God wholeheartedly, we will remain in the wilderness and be constantly prodded by the religious question. Temptation will hang in the balance until we make a definite decision and stand for or against God's Word.

Another area which causes problems is envy. Recall the story in Genesis chapter 4 about Cain and Abel? Cain's jealousy of his brother caused God to diagnose his condition, warn him, and give him a promise: "Sin is waiting to attack you, but you can conquer it! If you obey me and do what you should . . . your face will be bright with joy" (*see* Genesis 4:6, 7).

Then, I am sure, God withdrew Cain's consciousness of His presence. Along came the religious question: "Look at your brother. He's favored instead of you. Why don't you get rid of him, then God will have to pay attention to your sacrifices instead of his . . . ."

Envy is a dangerous seed. When our pride is hurt, we envy and are angry, and the seed of murder begins growing in our hearts. We all know the pangs of envy. A friend gets a promotion we had hoped for—our neighbor gets a new car—teacher pays more attention to our friend—Dad brags on our little brother. We all know anger—and I believe that there is the seed of murder in every human heart.

Cain chose to disobey God, and murdered his brother. What will be our choice when envy invades our consciousness? God's promise to us is the same as His promise to Cain: "You can conquer the evil that would destroy you. If you obey me and do what you should, your face will be bright with joy."

Joseph is another Old Testament character who was given a promise and faced many problems before coming into his provision. His story is recorded in Genesis chapters 37–50. After his dreams in which he was shown that all his brothers, his mother and his father would bow before him, Joseph found himself sold into slavery by his jealous brothers. Egypt became his eventual destination, and here, too, he met up with problems. One of these problems presented temptation through the wife of the captain of Pharaoh's guard.

Even though Joseph resisted Potiphar's wife, you can be sure he was having his own struggle with the religious questions: "Why don't you do as she suggests, Joseph? Why do you worry about sinning against God? God isn't doing anything for you. Potiphar's wife is an influential woman. Maybe she can help you to get free. Besides, Joseph, she's attractive and she is willing. What do you have to lose?"

But Joseph made his decision to obey God. There came other compromising situations, but the decision to obey God was maintained and we know that in the end God's original promise was fulfilled. He became keeper of the storehouses of Egypt, and during the years of famine his entire family *did* come and bow down to him.

Joseph came through the problem standing on the naked word of God in the midst of confusing, misleading, and difficult circumstances. There were things in his heart that needed to be put to the test. When you are tempted, don't blame it on the devil. He will only be allowed to come around as long as you need him. If you are drawn away from God, it will be by your *own* lust or desires.

One incident that stands out in my memory happened when I was a very young minister teaching in a Bible college. A man came to me with a tempting proposition. He said, "I need some money to buy five used cars to resell. I'll give you one of the cars free and clear if you will sign my note." Immediately I felt impressed that God didn't want me to sign that note. He would provide a car for me some other way.

God withdrew my consciousness of His presence and my old car began to look even older—the thought of a new car looked better all the time. I went home to my wife and said, "Judy, we ought to sign this." Her reply was, "The Lord tells me we shouldn't."

The religious questions came: "Who is head of this house? Who makes the decisions?" She succumbed—we signed the note—I didn't get the car I had been promised, and we were transferred to another Bible college.

Some months later I returned on a visit and walked into the local bank to greet my friend there. I was shocked to have him say to me, "Bob, I've been looking for you. . . ."

Yes—the car salesman had gone default on his payments—my name was on the papers—I had to assume financial responsibility for the debt. My reputation and my Christian witness were marred. But God had taught me a lesson!

In my heart had been the desire to get something for nothing. Many of us are vulnerable here. In God's purpose He could have provided me with a new car. But first He wanted to expose that little something lurking inside me. God wanted to bring it out into the open so that I could have an opportunity to turn it over to Him.

Before I could come into my provision, God had to expose me to temptation—that delicate balance between God, Satan, and my own nature. In this case, I failed the test because my own desire for a new car was stronger than my willingness to obey God's instructions. The result was another lap around the mountain—and an extended stay in the wilderness!

Is it becoming increasingly clear to you that before we can move into our promised land we must be prepared? And is the goodness of God becoming more evident to you in some circumstances which you have faced? What strength and assurance we can gain as our eyes are opened to the possibilities that are ours as we move out into the promises of God.

8

What Is the Promised Land?

Anyone who embarks on a deeper-than-surface reading of the Bible will soon discover the promised land in chapter 8 of the Book of Romans. We have already discussed some of the features of our promised land. It is not primarily a geographical location as in Exodus but a physical and spiritual reality. It is a place of rest where we have ceased from our own labors and are able to enjoy the provisions God has made for us. It is a land where we will dwell in cities we didn't build, enjoy fruit from orchards we didn't plant, drink water from wells we didn't dig. The physical provisions of the promised land include material possessions, health—all that we need for meeting the demands of the day. But these come about as a direct result of the spiritual provision God has made possible. When we possess the spiritual reality of the promised land, the milk and honey (an abundance of all we need) will flow.

The spiritual reality of our promised land is described in

Romans 8. Here is the assurance that we, as Christians, may live a life without guilt and condemnation—a life as joint heirs with Christ. All things may work out for our best. God will give us freely of all things—we can be more than conquerors through Him—and nothing can ever separate us from God's love in Christ. The entire chapter is a tremendous declaration of the victorious Christian life God has made available to us.

A friend once told me, "Most people *know* about Romans 8, but I *live* there." This is God's desire for us. He wants every one of the provisions of that chapter to function in our lives daily. We may learn to recite it from memory, but that will not insure our inhabiting the land of plenty and overflowing. How do we get there?

We go back again to our Law of the Four *Ps*. We have learned to look for a promise, principle and problem prior to the provision. In the Book of Romans, this pattern is demonstrated. Look at the chart below. Seen in this perspective, the four chapters fall into line with amazing clarity. They should be studied in sequence. Here we will merely focus on the key verses.

PROMISE	PRINCIPLE	PROBLEM	PROVISION
Chapter 5	Chapter 6	Chapter 7	Chapter 8

The Promise

For if, because of one man's trespass (lapse, offense) death reigned through that one, much more surely will those who receive [God's] overflowing grace (unmerited favor) and the free gift of righteousness (putting them into right standing with Himself) reign as kings in life through the One, Jesus Christ . . . .　　　　　Romans 5:17 AMPLIFIED

Here is our promise: We will reign as kings in this life.
The promise is for right now—not for some future date when
Christ returns. We are to reign over the circumstances in
which we find ourselves—at home—work—in school—every-
where. We are to reign amidst conflict, confusion, and problems.

The Principle

How the promise is to become reality is already indicated:
We are to "reign" *through* the One, Jesus Christ. Chapter
6 spells out in detail both *why* and *how* this is possible.
First the *why:*

> For you have become a part of him [Christ], and so you
> *died* with him, so to speak, and now you share his new life
> and shall rise as he did. Your old evil desires were nailed
> to the cross with him; that part of you that loves to sin was
> crushed and fatally wounded, so that your sin-loving body
> is no longer under sin's control, no longer *needs* to be slave
> to sin.   Romans 6:5, 6

Our lives as reigning kings have been made possible by
what Christ has already done for us. His substitutionary
death for us is a past reality, an established fact. By accepting what He has done for us personally, we are indeed dead
in the sense that our natural, sin-loving self no longer rules
over us. We no longer need to be slaves of sin; that is we
have been given the ability to choose. Now the option is
ours, and the principle tells us *how* we can use it:

> So look upon your old sin nature as dead and unresponsive
> to sin, and instead be alive to God, alert to him, through
> Jesus Christ our Lord. Do not let sin control your puny body
> any longer; do not give in to its sinful desires. Do not let any

part of your bodies become tools of wickedness, to be used
for sinning; but give yourself completely to God—every part
of you—for you are back from death and you want to be
tools in the hand of God, to be used for his good purpose.
vs. 11–13

Notice the action words: *look* upon, *be* alive, do not *let*,
do not *give* in, *give* yourself completely, *to be used* by God.
We are told to do basically two things. *Refuse* to respond in
the old way to sinful desires; and *give* ourselves totally to
God.

Don't you realize you can choose your own master? You can
choose sin (with death) or else obedience (with acquittal).
The one to whom you offer yourself—he will take you and
be your master and you will be his slave . . . just as you
used to be slaves to all kinds of sin, so now you must let
yourself be slaves to all that is right and holy.   vs. 16, 19

How do we become slaves to all that is right and holy? It
is easier said than done! Most of us start out by trying to be
good and soon discover that it doesn't work. The principle
is *not* trying to keep the law. God has given us another
method, and Paul wants to make this absolutely clear.

Now you need no longer worry about . . . the laws because
you "died" while in their captivity, and now you can really
serve God, not in the old way, mechanically obeying a set
of rules, but in the new way [with all of your hearts and
minds].   Romans 7:6

Paul tells us that God has provided a new way for us to
do His will, a new way to live within His law. We have seen
the principle explained. We are to actively resist evil desires,

and just as actively give ourselves wholeheartedly to God and *Christ will fulfill the law for us!*

Jesus said this:

> Don't misunderstand why I have come—it isn't to cancel the law of Moses and the warnings of the prophets. No, I came to fulfill them, and to make them all come true. With all the earnestness I have I say: Every law in the Book will continue until its purpose is achieved. And so if anyone breaks the least commandment, and teaches others to, he shall be the least in the Kingdom of Heaven. But those who teach God's laws *and obey them* shall be great in the Kingdom of Heaven.   Matthew 5:17–19

Jesus came to fulfill the law and make it come true *in us!* When Paul said we are free from the law's demands, he never meant to imply that the law was not valid anymore. He only meant that we need not struggle to keep the law in our own strength, because now we can put ourselves into God's hands and *let* Christ fulfill the law in our lives. This is the same kind of provision Moses talked about: cities we don't build . . . . Sound familiar? The cities are still built and the wells dug and the laws kept—by God's power, not our own.

The principle remains the same: We must *let* God do for us what we cannot possibly do for ourselves, and that includes keeping His law.

The Problem

The problem is put between the principle and the provision in order to reveal any tendency in us to do our own thing instead of abiding by God's instructions. The problem Paul describes is a common one for all of us. It is what happens once we've become aware of God's will and find ourselves incapable of doing it.

It seems to be a fact of life that when I want to do what is right, I inevitably do what is wrong. I love to do God's will so far as my new nature is concerned, but there is something else deep within me, in my lower nature, that is at war with my mind and wins the fight and makes me a slave to the sin that is still within me. In my mind I want to be God's willing servant but instead I find myself still enslaved to sin. So you see how it is: my new life tells me to do right, but the old nature that is still inside me loves to sin. Oh, what a terrible predicament I'm in! Who will free me from my slavery to this deadly lower nature? Romans 7:21–24

We know God's will, and we want to do it, but we can't. What did the problem reveal in Paul? A tendency to want to keep the law in his own strength. Paul was once a Pharisee. He knew all about using will power to keep the rules and regulations. You and I are self-willed people, once set on being "good" in our own strength. This is the most subtle of all rebellions—the desire to earn our own salvation—to be able to say, "Look at me. I'm keeping the law. I am loving —good—don't smoke—steal—commit adultery." The dangerous trap of rule-keeping will keep us from ever enjoying the fulfillment of the law in the promised land.

To reveal any hidden "Pharisee," or rule-keeper, in our hearts, God places us in situations where our own efforts at being good, fair, or loving will hopelessly fail. I have always desired to be a good father and a loving husband, but didn't know how. When I have wanted to be patient, pure, honest —then I found it impossible in my own strength. There have also been times when I wanted my family and neighbors to see a Christlike nature in me, and I have struggled to overcome the personal failures I know are unfit for someone who is supposed to "reign in this life."

I have seen other Christians in this same battle. I know

there are millions who struggle with their hidden envy, pride, resentment, covetousness, or other powerful tendencies that keep them bound and suffering in the wilderness of their problems. I know a good man in an evangelical church who cannot conquer his smoking habit. His church believes that Christians shouldn't smoke and as a result he hasn't dared to go to a service for several years because of his guilt and shame.

What can we do in this predicament? We know what God wants us to do but aren't able to do it. Listen to Paul's victory cry, ". . . Thank God! It has been done by Jesus Christ our Lord. He has set me free" (Romans 7:25). The only way to come through the problem into the provision is to let Jesus Christ do it for us. This is the principle Paul embraced. When we find ourselves in the problem, we must apply the principle we have learned.

Step One: Recognize and admit our own failure. "Lord, I'm torn by the temptation to lie on my income tax statement. Your law tells me that lying and stealing is sin, and so I know I am a sinner."

Step Two: Resist the pull of the wrong desire. "Lord, I don't *want* to cheat on my income tax. I *want* to obey the authorities You have placed over me."

Step Three: Turn yourself over to God to be used for His purpose. "Lord, I recognize I cannot obey You in my own strength. I turn myself and my financial situation over to You and ask that You enable me to fill out this return with the absolute honesty that only Christ can give as He lives in me and I in Him."

Letting Jesus do God's perfect will in us and through us is the *only way it can be done.*

The Provision

When our knowledge and practice of the principle has become tested and refined through the problem, we are able to enter the promised land—in this case, chapter 8 of Romans.

When the second generation Israelites entered Canaan, they found that each piece of the land had to be possessed separately. In other words, the principles and the problem had to come before each individual section of land could become theirs. In our individual Christian experience, we have to possess "the land" in the same manner.

In the first four verses of chapter 8, we have *three "pieces"* of our promised inheritance:

> So there is now *no condemnation* awaiting those who belong to Christ Jesus. For the power of the life-giving Spirit—and this power is mine through Christ Jesus—has freed me from the vicious circle of sin and death. We aren't saved from sin's grasp by knowing the commandments of God, because we can't and don't keep them; but God put into effect a different plan to save us. He sent his own Son in a human body like ours—except that ours are sinful—and destroyed sin's control over us by giving himself as a sacrifice for our sins. So now we can obey God's laws if we follow after the Holy Spirit and no longer obey the old evil nature within us.

1. We can live without condemnation.

2. We can be free from the vicious circle of sin and death.

3. We can be able to obey God's laws!

These can become spiritual realities as we apply the principle, resist our old nature, submit to God, and let Christ live in us and for us.

The problem will confront us with the temptation to do otherwise. The religious question will be aimed at us: "What do you mean, no condemnation! You're guilty and you know it. You're not good enough, you're not free from sin, and you certainly aren't obeying God's laws! You better try a little harder to be good." If we crumple up and submit to the guilt—seek to pray more—study more—strive to please— we are forced to take another lap around the mountain.

Instead of giving in to our guilt feelings, we may practice God's principle and respond, "Sure I am guilty. But Christ is without guilt, and it is His life in me that gives me right standing with God. I want to do God's will. I won't give in to my old doubts and guilt-feelings. I trust Jesus to change me. I am *not* under condemnation. I am free from the vicious circle of sin and death, and I am obeying God's law in Christ—and this regardless of how often I slip or how guilty I feel." With this response, we will soon come to experience the reality of freedom from guilt and condemnation.

There are twenty other "pieces" of land included in our inheritance as presented in Romans 8. We shall look briefly at each of these, thus getting some idea of the wonderful provisions that are ours for the taking.

4. We can be God-pleasers.

> Those who let themselves be controlled by their lower nature live only to please themselves, but those who follow after the Holy Spirit find themselves doing things that please God. v. 5

Ever since becoming a Christian, I have *wanted* to please God and I have discovered (the hard way—resulting in many laps around the problem) that I cannot possibly please God no matter how hard I try. Here God has provided a way for us. If we follow His instructions, we'll *find ourselves* doing things that please Him, quite effortlessly.

5. *We can have life and soul-peace.*

> Now the mind of the flesh [which is sense and reason without the Holy Spirit] is death—death that comprises all the miseries arising from sin, both here and hereafter. But the mind of the (Holy) Spirit is life and soul-peace [both now and forever].   v. 6 AMPLIFIED

How we all long for peace! Soul-peace is a peace that comes through our spirit to saturate our whole being—personality —mind—emotions. It means peace instead of frustration, tension, worry, or restlessness. It means quietness in the midst of our turbulent world. It is meant to be ours in Christ.

6. *The indwelling Holy Spirit can control us.*

> . . . You are controlled by your new nature if you have the Spirit of God living in you. (And remember that if anyone doesn't have the Spirit of Christ living in him, he is not a Christian at all.)   v. 9

We know from experience that it is possible to be a Christian, indwelt by the Holy Spirit—and yet not let the Holy Spirit control our lives. Control by the Holy Spirit is not an automatic feature of the Christian life. It can only come when we give up self-will, resist the control of our lower nature, and turn ourselves over to Christ. This is not done once and for all by a single decision, but must be repeated daily—often in the heat of a problem.

7. The Spirit can quicken our mortal bodies.

> And if the Spirit of God who raised up Jesus from the dead
> lives in you, he will make your dying bodies live again after
> you die, by means of this same Holy Spirit living within you.
>
> v. 11

This is not only a promise of life after death, but rather a
promise of physical "quickening" or divine provision for our
physical sickness and weakness. He is saying that our puny
mortal bodies can be quickened, given a new life, a new
surge of health and energy *right now*.

8. We can put to death the evil deeds of our body.

> . . . if through the power of the (Holy) Spirit you are
> habitually putting to death—making extinct, deadening—the
> [evil] deeds prompted by the body, you shall (really and
> genuinely) live forever.   v. 13 AMPLIFIED

Do you see how it is done? The principle is at work when we
habitually put to death (resist and deny) the old habits and
turn ourselves over to Christ instead.

9. We can be led by the Spirit of God.

> For all who are led by the Spirit of God are sons of God. v. 14

10. We can know the Spirit of adoption.

> For [the Spirit which] you have now received [is] not a
> spirit of slavery to put you once more in bondage to fear,
> but you have received the Spirit of adoption—the Spirit

producing sonship—in [the bliss of] which we cry Abba!
[That is,] Father!   v. 15 AMPLIFIED

11. The Spirit can tell us that we are His child.

For his Holy Spirit speaks to us deep in our hearts and tells
us that we really are God's children.   v. 16

This assurance is provided for us, but you can imagine the
problem and the religious questions putting it to the test!

12. We can be joint heirs with Christ.

And since we are his children, we will share his treasures—
for all God gives to his Son Jesus is now ours too. . . .   v. 17

13. Glorious freedom from sin.

For on that day [when God will resurrect His children]
thorns and thistles, sin, death and decay—the things that
overcame the world against its will at God's command—will
all disappear and the world around us will share in the
glorious freedom from sin which God's children enjoy.
                                          vs. 20, 21

Paul is talking about the complete freedom from sin we will
enjoy in the future, after the resurrection. But he also speaks
of a *substantial* freedom from sin which God's children can
enjoy even today.

14. The redemption of our bodies.

And even we Christians, although we have the Holy Spirit
within us as a foretaste of future glory, also groan to be re-

leased from pain and suffering. We, too, wait anxiously for
that day when God will give us full rights as his children,
including the new bodies he has promised us—bodies that
will never be sick again and will never die.   v. 23

The last two provisions are the only ones we can't experience
fully until the day when Christ comes again. Nevertheless,
there is even now some measure of fulfillment here. Even
our present-day, dying bodies can experience greater life
than most of us know today.

15. The Spirit can help with our daily problems and prayers.

And in the same way—by our faith—the Holy Spirit helps us
with our daily problems and in our praying. For we don't
even know what we should pray for, nor how to pray as we
should; but the Holy Spirit prays for us with such feeling
that it cannot be expressed in words.   v. 26

16. We can know that everything happens for our good.

And we know that all that happens to us is working for our
good if we love God and are fitting into his plans.   v. 28

Many Christians quote this verse, but are unable to see their
problems as part of God's plan for their good. God's plan is
to bring us from the promise into the provision. The problem doesn't pop up to thwart God's intentions, but is an inevitable part of His plan. *All* that happens to us is meant to
work for our good, including the things that we have habitually called bad. This springs from our old nature, our reason,
and understanding without the Holy Spirit's enlightening.
We must deliberately resist these old thought patterns. Con-

fess them as sin, ask God to take them away and replace them with the ability to look at *all* things as part of His good plan. This ability is ours in Christ.

17. *We can become conformed to Christ's image.*

> For from the very beginning God decided that those who came to him—and all along he knew who would—should become like his Son, so that His Son would be the First, with many brothers.   v. 29

You and I cannot live Christlike lives by trying to be like Him. We can only be like Him to the degree that He lives His life in us.

18. *We can know that God is always on our side.*

> What can we say to such wonderful things as these? If God is on our side, who can ever be against us?   v. 31

Have you ever felt that you were alone against the whole world? Moses faced the whole nation of Israel who wanted to stone him and return to the fleshpots of Egypt. But God was with Moses, and God always constitutes the majority of One. He has made the provision to be always on our side, but in the middle of the problem it may not seem that way!

19. *God will freely give us all things.*

> Since he did not spare even his own Son for us but gave him up for us all, won't he also surely give us everything else?
>   v. 32

20. Christ will plead our cause.

> Who then will condemn us? Will Christ? *No!* For he is the
> one who died for us and came back to life again for us and
> is sitting at the place of highest honor next to God, pleading
> for us there in heaven.   v. 34

Christ is pleading our cause, but we cannot receive the full
benefits of this provision until we yield ourselves to Him. If
we remain stubborn in our self-sufficiency, we cannot receive what Christ has won for us.

21. Nothing can keep Christ's love from us.

> Who then can ever keep Christ's love from us? When we
> have trouble or calamity, when we are hunted down or
> destroyed, is it because he doesn't love us anymore? And if
> we are hungry, or penniless, or in danger, or threatened with
> death, has God deserted us? No, for the Scripture tells us
> that for his sake we must be ready to face death at every
> moment of the day—we are like sheep awaiting slaughter.
>   vs. 35, 36

This list of circumstances sounds like a very inclusive description of any wilderness area we might encounter. The
religious question in the midst of temptation will always
suggest that this is proof that God has left us or doesn't love
us. On the contrary, it is only *through* very difficult circumstances that we can learn to rely on God's constant presence
and never-ending love.

22. We can be more than conquerors.

> Yet amid all these things we are more than conquerors *and*
> gain a surpassing victory through Him who loved us.
>   v. 37 AMPLIFIED

The victory is always ours through Christ, because it simply cannot be won any other way.

23. *Nothing can separate us from God's love.*

> For I am convinced that nothing can ever separate us from his love. Death can't, and life can't. The angels won't, and all the powers of hell itself cannot keep God's love away. Our fears for today, our worries about tomorrow, or where we are—high above the sky, or in the deepest ocean—nothing will ever be able to separate us from the love of God demonstrated by our Lord Jesus Christ when he died for us.   v. 38

Here is our promised land, and we are meant to live there. Not just in one area of it—and not for just a visit while we feel spiritual—but always. Many Christians share Paul's problem in chapter 7. They know what God wants them to do but flounder in the problem—unable to obey.

The answer to the predicament is to quit trying so hard on our own and let Jesus do it for us instead. When we learn to apply that principle to all of our problems, we can become permanent residents in the promised land!

9

Christ in Temptation

The Bible tells us that Jesus Christ was tempted in every respect as we are and it is unrealistic to think that His temptation differed from ours.

Jesus Christ was given the promise, taught the principle, then God withdrew from His Son the consciousness of His presence, and Jesus was exposed to all the forces of hell. All the religious questions Satan is capable of suggesting were thrown at our Lord and Saviour. The temptation of Jesus would not have been real had it not contained the possibility of failure. Anything less would have been contrary to the principles of God. The Israelites were chosen of God to enter the Promised Land, yet they failed to come into their full provision. Jesus Christ, God's only Son, *could,* conceivably, have failed as well.

The Gospels tell of Jesus' temptation in the wilderness, and it is interesting to note the chronological order of events. The temptation occurred immediately *after* Jesus had been baptized in the Jordan River and had been filled with the Holy Spirit as well, and *before* He entered His ministry as Messiah. Failure in the problem wouldn't have changed the fact that He was God's Son who had been filled with the Holy Spirit, but it would have adversely affected His role as Messiah, His provision.

Many Christians say, "Oh, if I could only be full of the Holy Spirit, then I wouldn't have any more problems." Take another look at the life of Jesus! God *wants* every one of us to be emptied of self and *filled* with His Holy Spirit. But when you pray to be filled with the Holy Spirit, don't expect your problems to all melt away; instead expect *new* problems. This is a necessary part of the package. The infilling of the Holy Spirit is the potential, or the promise. It must be put to the test before we can safely come into our provision.

The same principle holds true when a spaceship is built. Before it can take off for outer space, it is tested under full power to see if all systems are go. If any defects show up during the test, the part is repaired or exchanged. When God fills us with His Holy Spirit, we are put through the test to see if our systems are go. Then we are ready to be launched on the mission He has for us.

Luke tells us that Jesus came to the Jordan River where John was preaching and baptizing. Jesus asked to be baptized, and we know that John didn't think this was proper:

"I am the one who needs to be baptized by you," [he said.] But Jesus said, "Please do it, for I must do all that is right."
Matthew 3:14, 15

Commentators suggest that in presenting Himself for baptism, Jesus fulfilled righteousness. When He later allowed

Himself to be driven into the wilderness to be tempted, it was so that His righteousness could be tried.

Jesus knew that He had come to fulfill God's law and the writings of the prophets. He was thoroughly familiar with every word of God written in the Scriptures. These were His *principles*—willingness to obey what God had said.

There are only a few glimpses of Jesus' childhood and youth in the Scriptures, but they are sufficient to establish that He was exceptionally well acquainted with the Scriptures.

> There the child became a strong, robust lad, and was known for his wisdom beyond his years; and God poured out his blessings on him. . . . [When Jesus was twelve years old He stayed in Jerusalem and His parents had to come and look for Him.] Three days later they finally discovered him. He was in the Temple, sitting among the teachers of the Law, discussing deep questions with them and amazing everyone with his understanding and answers.   Luke 2:40, 46, 47

Jesus was baptized by John (Luke 3:21, 22) and we read:

> . . . and as he was praying, the heavens opened and the Holy Spirit in the form of a dove settled upon him and a voice from heaven said: "You are my much loved Son, yes, my delight."

There is general agreement among theologians that this double baptism of water and the Holy Spirit constituted the preparation for Jesus' messianic ministry. But the preparation wasn't complete. Instead of setting out immediately on His life-giving mission, we find that

> Then Jesus, full of the Holy Spirit, left the Jordan River, being urged [Mark's record says *driven*] by the Spirit out

into the barren wastelands of Judea, where Satan tempted
him for forty days. . . .   Luke 4:1

A Christian who experiences an infilling, or a Baptism of
the Holy Spirit, may be told by well meaning but misled
fellow-believers that he is now ready and prepared for "doing a great work for God." He may be totally unprepared for
what comes next—a trip to the wilderness and a confrontation with the enemy. In the problems and confusion following, many Christians have despaired, and then concluded
that the whole experience with the Holy Spirit was a product
of his own imagination and the beginning of all his troubles.

Jesus was in the wilderness, alone with Satan, for forty
days and nights without eating; and the Bible says he was
hungry. The Scriptures do not state specifically that God
withdrew the consciousness of His presence from Jesus, but
I think we can be absolutely certain that He did. Had Jesus
been able to sense God's presence, the temptation would
have been a farce. We know that it was deadly serious business where His messianic role and the salvation of mankind
was at stake. Luke chapter 4 records the conflict.

Satan's first attack came in the realm of physical provision. It had to do with Jesus' very real hunger pains—His
feelings of fatigue and discomfort. Satan presented the religious question, "*If* you are God's Son, tell this stone to become a loaf of bread" (v. 3).

Jesus *knew* He was the Son of God and perfectly capable
of turning that stone into bread. He was also extremely hungry. The miracle could easily be justified. But more than
hunger was at stake here. Satan was suggesting that Jesus use
His power to satisfy His own need; and he was also implying
that His greatest need was for bread.

There is a fine line between selfishness and a legitimate

love of self which Jesus told us to have (Mark 12:31): "You must love others as much as yourself." Jesus had the authority to ask for blessings for others as well as for Himself, but He had come to offer Himself as the bread of life to those who hungered for more than physical satisfactions.

The temptation comes to every believer to use his authority to ask for blessings from a selfish motive. Satan suggests that this is justifiable and reasonable. ("You need a bigger house—a better job—more money. God will be glorified when you prosper; so go ahead and ask for those stones to be turned into bread!")

Jesus answered Satan, "It is written in the Scriptures: 'Other things in life are much more important than bread!'" Jesus chose to remain hungry but obedient to God's Word, rather than to satisfy his own physical need by provoking God. He quoted from the Scripture account of the Israelites in the wilderness; they had been tested in the same way and had failed. Listen as Moses reminded the people of God's goodness and desires for them:

Do you remember how the Lord led you through the wilderness for all those forty years, humbling you and testing you to find out how you would respond and whether or not you would really obey him? Yes, he humbled you by letting you go hungry and then feeding you with manna, a food previously unknown to both you and your ancestors. He did it to help you realize that food isn't everything, and that real life comes by obeying every command of God.

Deuteronomy 8:2, 3

The Israelites gave in to temptation and begged for bread. As a consequence they were unable to enter their

Promised Land. Jesus in the wilderness won the victory—and the provision!

The second temptation is recorded for us this way:

> Then Satan took him up and revealed to him all the kingdoms of the world in a moment of time; and the devil told him, "I will give you all these splendid kingdoms and their glory—if you will only get down on your knees and worship me."   Luke 4:5

Who and what a man worships is the final test of his heart. Satan knew Jesus' identity and His appointed role as Messiah and ultimate ruler of the earth. But he also knew that Jesus had been asked to go the way of the cross, the way of suffering, rejection, and death. Now he offered Him a *compromise*—an easy way out!

I am convinced that this was no easy temptation for Jesus to face. He was alone in the wilderness, tired and hungry, and not conscious of the presence of God. Had He been, the temptation to worship anyone else would have been completely meaningless. At this point, Satan appeared before Him in all his power, beauty, and light. In 2 Corinthians 11:14, he is described as "an angel of light," and his appearance can be both beautiful and appealing.

A man I know had reached a crisis point in his Christian commitment and went away to fast and pray. After three days alone in a hotel room, he sensed the presence of God with him in a glorious way. The man was kneeling in prayer when it happened, and he became so overwhelmed with awe that he put his face down in the rug. There he stayed; and after a while the sense of God's presence lifted from him.

He remained with his face down and eyes tightly closed. Suddenly he "saw" a man standing before him. He was the most beautiful person he had ever seen and was surrounded by an aura of light. A strong desire to worship the beautiful apparition swept over him, and he could hear a voice, strong and smooth saying, "If you worship me, I will give you a powerful healing ministry. All the world will know you!" The urge to comply with the suggestion was so great that it pulled at his entire being. Finally, deep down in the recesses of his soul a word formed—*Jesus.* He struggled to make his lips utter it—and at last he spoke aloud that Name. The moment the word passed his lips, the vision of the beautiful figure disappeared from behind his closed eyelids.

The temptation to worship the powerful prince of this world (2 Corinthians 4:4) is not to be taken lightly. The temptation to compromise—to pay homage to the world in order to gain a desirable end—is a subtle one and must be faced by each of us. Jesus told us, "No man can serve two masters . . ." (Matthew 6:24 KJV). Compromise is not possible in the realm of worship. To worship is to declare that God alone is worthy. To worship another creature or thing, in order to gain an end, is the very essence of rejecting God's throne rights.

Jesus' reply to the second temptation was, "We must worship God and him alone, so it is written in the Scriptures" (Luke 4:8). Again He referred to the Scripture record of the Israelites in the wilderness. They had been taught the same principle from Mount Sinai: "I am Jehovah your God who liberated you from slavery in Egypt. You may worship no other god than me" (Exodus 20:2, 3).

Exposed to temptation when they no longer sensed God's presence with them, the Israelites disobeyed this command and worshiped the golden image of the calf. Again, where they failed and lost their provision, Jesus obeyed God's Word and won.

Finally, Satan tried a third time, using a quotation from the Scriptures (Psalm 91:11) to pose the religious question:

> Then Satan took him to Jerusalem to a high roof of the Temple and said, "If you are the Son of God, jump off! For the Scriptures say that God will send his angels to guard you and to keep you from crashing to the pavement below!" Jesus replied, "The Scriptures also say, 'Do not put the Lord your God to a foolish test.'"   Luke 4:9–12

We note that Satan took his scriptural reference out of context. This is perhaps the most dangerous form of temptation for a sincere Christian—the suggestion that there is scriptural authority for the proposed action. Satan suggested to Jesus that He do something spectacular to demonstrate His supernatural power. Miracles were to be a part of His ministry. To jump off the Temple roof and be carried to the pavement below by God's angels could certainly launch His mission in a spectacular way.

What was wrong with the suggestion? Wasn't it true that God had promised to give His angels charge over Jesus? Wouldn't His jump demonstrate the glory and power of God to the people of Jerusalem?

First, consider the suggested action: to jump off the Temple roof. It was spectacular, unusual, unnatural—and quite unnecessary. God seldom works in spectacular, unusual ways —and never in unnatural or unnecessary ways. When Jesus fed the five thousand, He didn't do it in a spectacular or unnatural way. He *could* have turned the stones on the hillside into bread. Instead He quietly took the loaves and fishes, thanked God for them, and proceeded to divide them among the hungry. The whole process appeared so natural and simple that those who watched hardly realized a miracle was taking place.

Those who have witnessed or experienced physical healings often express amazement at how *natural and simple* the whole process appears to be. Two testimonies show this to be true. First is a woman who had suffered many years with crippling arthritis; secondly, one who was born with one blind eye and the other seriously defective.

(1) "I had prayed for God to heal me and knew that in His great love, He would. One afternoon I was home alone, rejoicing in His love and concern. Suddenly my hands simply straightened out. All pain vanished, and before my eyes my fingers relaxed and looked and felt as if I had never had any discomfort or disease. It all happened so *naturally* that I caught myself thinking that the years of sickness had never been. I had expected God to heal in a more spectacular way."

(2) "I wanted to serve God as a Christian teacher and I knew I could serve Him better as a "seeing" teacher than a blind one. Finally, I got up the courage to ask God to heal me. I went to bed that night after praying and put my glasses on the nightstand. Next morning, I thought the sunshine seemed unusually bright, and the tree outside my window greener than before. I put on my glasses, as I always do first thing in the morning. To my surprise, everything looked fuzzy! Taking them off again, everything was clear! God had simply healed my sight while I slept. Being healed was the most *normal* thing I ever experienced."

We are just naturally drawn to the spectacular. Violence and drama occupy center stage in the secular world. Christians are drawn, too, toward the spectacular in demonstrations of God's power. This is how sincere believers are drawn into fanaticism of one kind or another. Claiming isolated Scripture texts as God's direction for their action, they look for strange and unusual so-called miracles as signs of spirituality.

A woman who had recently experienced a fresh encounter with the Holy Spirit came to my office deeply concerned that she might have disobeyed God in a particular incident. She had been attending a funeral where she had nearly been overcome with an urge to jump up during the service and command the body in the casket to come back to life. She had resisted and now was tormented by guilt.

"Did I disobey God?" she asked. "Jesus raised the dead and the Bible tells us that we can do what He did."

God is able to raise the dead, even today. But He will not use a believer to perform such a miracle without solid preparation. A fundamental part of the preparation is familiarity with the entire Scripture. We need to know the broad sweep of God's program here on earth. He will never ask us to do anything that is out of line with His character and total thrust.

This new Christian, unfamiliar with the whole Scripture, was a prime target for the temptation to "jump off the Temple roof." We read together the record of Jesus' temptation and His reply, and she came to see some of the workings of the tempter.

Let me give several checkpoints to help recognize whether or not an urge to do something which appears "spiritual" comes from God—Satan—or our own desires:

(1) Is it in line with God's total program as revealed in the Scripture? Does it reflect God's character of love and justice?

(2) Is it spectacular, unusual, or unnatural? If so, be careful. God usually works in simple, natural, and intelligible ways.

(3) Has God prepared you for it? God doesn't act on the spur of the moment: His Word and intentions are unchanging and eternal. When God wants you to do something, He will prepare you over a period of time, through Scripture, circumstances, and impressions. When the time for action comes, you will recognize that God has led you.

(4) Is it necessary? This may seem to be a superfluous question, but the temptation to engage in unnecessary activities "for the Lord" is a common one.

Returning to Jesus and Satan on the Temple roof, we hear the reply to the third temptation, "The Scriptures also say, 'Do not put the Lord your God to a foolish test.'" Again, we recognize a reference to the scriptural record of the Israelites in the wilderness. They had been warned *not* to put God to a foolish test (tempt Him). Again, the Israelites failed; they asked for a sign greater than He was pleased to give. They provoked Him and lost their provision.

Jesus was tempted in the same realms as the Israelites. Where they lost, He won. Throughout the temptations, He did what they had been instructed to do. He stood on the naked Word of God without the conscious awareness of God's presence. When we are tempted, we must do likewise.

The only way through the problem is total reliance on God and His Word. There can be no other assurance of help. God's Word is sufficient. It is, therefore, essential that we be sure of what God has told us in the first place. Nothing is more tragic than the Christian who stands on *a* word of

God—taken out of context and twisted by the master deceiver.

When Satan left Jesus in the wilderness, God sent angels to care for Him. This strengthens the fact that Jesus was in the wilderness *without* a sense of the presence of God. When the angels came to care for Him, the sense of God's concern, love, and presence returned: "then Jesus returned to Galilee, full of the Holy Spirit's power . . ." (v. 14).

Compare this statement with the one made before the wilderness experience (Luke 4:1 with Luke 4:14). After the testing in the wilderness, Jesus was full of the Holy Spirit's *power*. Now He was ready to enter into the provision—the ministry God had prepared for Him. Jesus was on the victory side of the problem and He could announce to the world that He had come to fulfill what the Scripture promised (Luke 16–21). Here is a portion of His statement:

> "The Spirit of the Lord is upon me; he has appointed me to preach the Good News to the poor; he has sent me to announce that captives shall be released and the blind shall see, that the downtrodden shall be freed from their oppressors, and that God is ready to give blessings to all who come to him . . . These Scriptures came true today!"
>
> Luke 4:18, 19, 21

We have reason to look at the church today and ask, "Where is the power Jesus promised the believers? Where is the ability to meet the need of the oppressed, the sick, the blind, and the brokenhearted?

Power as a promise isn't the same as power in action! Between the promise and the realization of power comes the principle and the problem. *Victory in the problem transforms the promise into power.*

If the church today lacks power, it isn't because God has withheld His promise or broken His Word, but because there are so few Christians who have come through the problem successfully. The power promised to the church is dissipated by repeated laps around the mountain.

Jesus withstood the temptations in the wilderness. Because He did, the way is open for us to do the same. We, too, can stand on the principle of God's naked Word and be prepared to receive the fullness of the power of the Holy Spirit. This power is promised to us, as believers, *not in our strength, but in His!*

10

Five Fiery Serpents

Temptation in the wilderness serves the purpose of exposing what is really in our hearts. This is necessary before we can have an honest and satisfactory relationship with God—and reach the maturity by which we enter into the provisions of the promised land.

Jesus taught His disciples to pray, "Don't bring us into temptation, but deliver us from the Evil One" (Matthew 6:13). Some theologians have questioned whether or not this verse belongs in the Bible. They are of the opinion that God doesn't lead anyone into temptation, and to ask Him *not* to do it clearly implies that He *might* possibly do it.

God *does* lead us into temptation in order to reveal what is in our hearts, and a valid interpretation of this Scripture would be, *Dear God, let there be nothing in my heart that would cause You to put me to the test.*

Wherever sin or confusion reigns, Satan has an open door.

There are three major wilderness areas where all of us must be tested to a greater or lesser degree. They are:

(1) Promiscuity—sexual immorality
(2) Greed—love of money
(3) Pride—ego problems.

We are going to look into the hearts of three men.

David

There was a little something in David's heart that caused God to expose him to the view of the beautiful Bathsheba bathing on her rooftop. David yielded to the temptation and suffered a painful lap through the problem.

David didn't perish in the problem. He saw and admitted his sin, repented, and was forgiven. But much harm was done. Bathsheba's husband was killed and the first child she bore David had to die.

Judas

Judas had a secret love of money. There is nothing evil about money in itself, contrary to what we are often led to believe. Jesus knew the secret of Judas's heart and deliberately exposed him to temptation by handing him the money bag.

Matthew, the ex-tax collector, would have been a much more likely treasurer. But Jesus knew that unless the weakness in Judas was exposed and faced through real temptation, Judas could never be a single-minded follower. His weakness had to be exposed—even at risk of total failure. We know the outcome of this problem—failure!

Saul

Saul's problem was pride. He erected a monument to himself after winning a battle—but he disobeyed God's command to kill all his enemies and their cattle (1 Samuel 15).

Samuel, the prophet, confronted King Saul with his sin and he refused to admit his disobedience until he was told that God would take way his kingship as a consequence. At last Saul confessed his sin. But he begged Samuel, "Oh, at least honor me before the leaders and before my people by going with me to worship the Lord your God" (v. 30). Saul was more concerned with his reputation than with his relationship to God. Pride can cause us to perish in the wilderness.

When our weakness (or sin) is exposed, we can either admit it, repent, and be cleansed and forgiven—as David was—or we can hide, cling to our reputation among our peers, and fail in the problem.

Satan will always come to suggest, "What do you think *they* would say if they knew? You better not admit to your weakness."

A man attending this series of teaching sessions came to me and said, "I've been fighting this thing since your first lecture. I have a problem but I'm afraid of what you're going to say when you hear it." I waited and watched the obvious torment on the man's face. He was a respectable Christian businessman. Finally he continued, "You see I've got these lustful thoughts and I can't get rid of them."

Once the words were uttered, he looked greatly relieved. I replied, "Brother, you know, I think you are very normal. God is permitting you to struggle with your problem to show you what is in your heart. Now that you've confessed it, ask God to forgive and cleanse your heart, and let Christ fill that area of your life."

Once the problem area is exposed and cleansed, you can face any temptation with ease. Along comes a pretty girl—an opportunity to cheat on your income tax—a chance to boost your ego—you can then say, "Thank You, Father. I don't need those things anymore. I depend on You!"

God has what I call a Ways and Means Committee in the wilderness especially assigned to bring out our weaknesses. Five fiery serpents came to tempt the Israelites in the wilderness and led them to perish there. In 1 Corinthians 10:6 AMPLIFIED Paul held them up as a serious warning to all of us: "Now these things are examples (warnings and admonitions) for us . . . ."

"[Don't] desire *or* crave *or* covet *or* lust after evil *and* carnal things as they did."

The Israelites craved meat, although they were being fed adequately every day with manna from heaven. They complained until God became angry. To teach them a lesson He sent enough for them to eat until they were nauseous.

A desire or craving for anything other than God amounts to a rejection of Him. To teach us, God may send an overabundance of what we crave. There is no more effective cure than to get sick on what we lust after! Unless we are cured of our inordinate desire for anything other than God and His purposes for us—spiritually, physically, and geographically—we will live a life of continual double-mindedness and dissatisfaction.

Your desire may be for a career. A friend of mine felt God's call to the ministry. But all of his life he had wanted to own a gas station. The desire was so strong he couldn't give it up. The cure was an overdose of service-station management!

You may have your mind set on living in a certain geographical location. Perhaps you live in Omaha, where God wants you. But inside, you cherish a persistent longing to live in San Francisco. God may permit the move because as long as you nurse that longing in your heart, you are incapable of experiencing the fullness of God's provision for you in Omaha.

Your desire may be for a thing or a place or a person. God will provide the opportunity to satisfy that desire, expose it to where you will either (1) give in to the desire and suffer continued laps in the problem, or (2) confess it, resist it, and choose to give your full allegiance to what God wants for you. Then you are ready to receive your provision.

IDOLATRY

"Do not be worshippers of false gods as some of them were . . ." (v. 7 AMPLIFIED).

Idolatry is lust and desire come to its maturity. Therefore, it poses a more serious threat than the first fiery serpent. We are told to "love the Lord your God with all your [mind and] heart and with your entire being and with all your might" (Deuteronomy 6:5 AMPLIFIED).

God knew the weakness in the heart of the Israelites and He permitted them to be exposed to temptation. God had commanded them to love and worship Him only and to keep from making any molten images. Then God withdrew from their conscious awareness of His presence through the person of His spokesman, Moses, as he went up on the mountain. Immediately the weakness in their hearts came to the surface with full force and they implored Aaron to make them a golden image of a calf. Why a calf?

The Bible prohibits the making of images—mental or metal—because an image takes away from God as the central object of our love. The molten calf represented the image of one of the gods of Egypt—the bull Osiris. The ex-slaves cherished the dream of Egypt in their hearts, and whenever they were confronted with a temptation in the wilderness, their first impulse was to go back to the fleshpots they had left behind. When Moses was absent, they wanted to go back to Egypt again; but they needed the calf as a sign to the Egyptians that they had withdrawn their allegiance from the invisible Jehovah and placed it with Osiris. This would keep them from being slain by the Egyptian army.

Idolatry always involves allegiance to something other than God, and often springs from a desire to be accepted by another group or person. It may start innocently enough when a Christian finds himself in the company of a new group of people he has secretly admired. They may not think much of Christianity, and along comes the temptation to hide his identity. Later follows the temptation to take on the signs of allegiance to their way of life (dress, talk, behavior, whatever is the "in" thing to do) in order to be accepted as one of the group. This applies to youth and adults alike!

If there is in your heart a secret desire to identify with something other than God, then temptation will come in the form of an opportunity to identify with your idol. God permits us to be tempted with opportunities because to go on with *divided loyalty* is a frustration—both to us and to Him.

Jesus told us, "No one who puts his hand to the plow and looks back [to the things behind] is fit for the kingdom of God" (Luke 9:62 AMPLIFIED). He who commits himself to God and becomes a worker in God's vineyard—and then looks back to the things of the past, finds himself unfit for the kingdom and consequently loses the spiritual provision and the joy God has promised.

If God calls you from being a business executive into the ministry—don't look back. If He brings you out of Buddhism—don't look back. You cannot compromise your wholehearted devotion to God. Our God requires full allegiance —or we are left with empty promises!

"We must not gratify evil desire *and* indulge in immorality as some of them did, and twenty-three thousand [suddenly] fell *dead* in a single day!" (1 Corinthians 10:8 AMPLIFIED).

The word fornication is all-inclusive—meaning all types of sexual sin, perversion, and promiscuity.

The Israelites ignored God's command and committed sexual sins with the women of Moab. They also joined them in idol worship. God's anger was roused and a plague struck down twenty-three thousand of their number.

God speaks out against immorality—not against sex. Unfortunately, many Christians have been led to believe that sex is "unspiritual and carnal"—something to be tolerated to reproduce. Nothing could be further from the truth. If God did not approve of sex, He would have invented another way to continue the human race. And we need to remind ourselves that God *created* Adam and Eve as sexual beings before sin entered the picture.

God intended the sexual relationship to be a form of intimate communication between man and wife, to be enjoyed by both of them. Sexual fulfillment and enjoyment is a part of the promised land God wants us to live in. We will be able to experience the fulfillment of that promise once we have learned the principle and come through the problem.

The Bible restricts all sexual activities to the confines of marital relationship. There is to be no before—or besides. This is part of the principle. It is not meant to rob us of joy but to guide us towards the fullness of joy that can only be experienced within the marriage. True sexual freedom can only be enjoyed in obedience to God's design. This is sexual liberation in the true sense of the word. Illegal sex, perversion, or sex outside of marriage is forbidden because God knows that such action brings suffering and despair.

Once I was called upon to counsel with a pastor and his wife who were deep in marital troubles. Over a long period of time, the pastor had been so busy that his wife had been left much alone. She felt neglected and unloved, both physically and emotionally. In this wilderness of loneliness, the fiery serpent of sexual immorality struck. She responded to the temptation and the result was the breakup of two Christian marriages involving seven children. Much heartbreak and loss of faith among the church members resulted.

The hidden weakness had been in the heart of the woman. God knew this and permitted exposure to temptation. Had she chosen to stand on God's command, the door would have opened for her into the promised land of fulfillment in her marriage. Instead, in the heat of temptation, she and her lover decided that their desire was great enough to warrant the sacrifice of all other considerations. As a consequence, they lost their personal share of God's provision.

TEMPTING GOD

"We should not tempt the Lord—try His patience, become a trial to Him, critically appraise Him and exploit His goodness—as some of them did . . ." (1 Corinthians 10:9 AMPLIFIED).

The Israelites complained in the wilderness and said they hated "the insipid manna" God had provided for them. As a result, God sent poisonous snakes among them and many were bitten and died.

We test God's patience when we demand more than the adequate supply He has given us. We tempt Him when we ask for a sign and He has already made clear what He wants us to do. We put Him to a foolish test when we ask Him to prove His power when He has already shown us enough to establish our faith.

When I was a student in Bible college, Judy and I and our baby daughter lived in a tiny trailer. Our monthly support was a veteran's check of eighty dollars per month, plus occasional gifts from concerned people. God's provision had always been exactly what we needed and I felt very secure in His love and concern for us.

Then one day the gifts stopped coming and my monthly check didn't arrive when it was due. In a few days we were almost out of food and I was concerned for my wife and child. I sat down to dinner (cream of wheat with canned milk without sugar) and came very close to complaining to God. I wanted to say, "What's the matter with You, Lord? Can't You take care of me while I'm here studying to be a minister of Your gospel?" Instead, I said to Judy, "I don't understand why the Lord *seems* to have failed us."

To my surprise, Judy laughed and replied, "I understand perfectly well. Remember last week we discussed *who* is providing for us? Is it the government with the veteran's check and those nice people with their gifts, or is it the Lord? I never had been convinced one way or the other, and I asked the Lord, *if* He was doing the providing, to please give me a sign by cutting off our supply."

I stared at my wife. Here she was tempting the Lord and,

as a result, I was eating cream of wheat without sugar—
which I detested! I asked, "Well, are you convinced now?"

She nodded and said, "I surely am, and I'll pray that God
releases the provision He's been holding back. I guess we
need about fifty dollars to restock our cupboard."

That evening we went to a meeting and when we returned
we found two boxes of groceries and an envelope with a
twenty-dollar bill in it. The food items were worth approxi-
mately thirty dollars and were exactly what we had planned
to buy. Judy accepted the provisions very matter-of-factly
and said, "Thank You, Lord," as she began putting the
groceries away.

Did we tempt the Lord? Yes, we did—because He had
promised to provide for us, and had given ample evidence
in the past that He was able to meet our needs. Putting Him
to the proof was an expression of doubt.

God knows what is in our hearts. If our desire to trust
Him is genuine—and yet we need a little reassurance—He
will respond with the sign we ask for. But the consequence
will be another lap—an extended period in the problem. God
wants to bring us to the place where we trust Him—without
obvious demonstrations or any additional proofs.

Gideon is an example of this. Judges chapter 6 gives the
account of his asking God for proof that He would be with
him and his men when they went out to battle. God had
already demonstrated His presence with an angel who per-
formed the miracle of lighting Gideon's fire with his stick.
We can understand his concern for there was much at stake.
God had asked him to lead a small army of men against a
strong enemy. God had promised to win the battle for them
but Gideon wanted to be double-sure that he was dealing
with God and not a figment of his own imagination. After

all, if Jehovah wasn't involved, Gideon and his men were as good as dead.

Gideon tested God—twice—by asking that He make a fleece of wool wet with dew on a dry ground, and later keep the fleece dry while the ground remained wet. Gideon knew he was in danger of bringing down God's anger by asking for these signs.

God knew that Gideon was willing to be obedient to His command *if* he could only be sure God was doing the commanding. Therefore, God was patient. But the warning is clear: Don't tempt God; don't test His patience; don't take advantage of His goodness. It is dangerous business. To tempt God shows doubt and dissatisfaction in our hearts.

MURMURING

"And don't murmur against God and his dealings with you as some of them did, for that is why God sent his Angel to destroy them" (1 Corinthians 10:10).

The Israelites' complaints had hardened into open rebellion. A revolt was started against Moses and God slew the rebels.

Murmuring is the most dangerous of all the fiery serpents in the wilderness. *A habit of complaining becomes a constant attitude of discontent.* We complain about circumstances, but "murmur" is directed against God.

The murmurer is always a pessimist. No matter what the future may look like, he always expects the worst. He looks for the economy to collapse—his health to fail—his marriage to break up—his children to go astray—and an earthquake to destroy the land.

The murmurer equates suffering with reality. He feels

that in this world sorrow is to be expected, while happiness is for fools and dreamers who don't know what life is all about. He feels that he has been treated unjustly by God, life, his wife, neighbors, boss—and so on. He demonstrates his negative attitude in a constant stream of criticism directed at everyone and everything: Prices are outrageous! the government corrupt! young people irresponsible! every other driver a fool, and there isn't a decent program on television anymore!

Like the Israelites in the wilderness, the murmurer looks back with longing to the past: "It was different when I was young—or when I lived in the country—or when we were first married." An attitude of murmuring sours everything it comes in touch with. Once our complaining has become habitual and causes our hearts to harden against God, it is almost impossible to break the cycle. It was the cause of the bleached bones in the wilderness.

Paul summed up his warnings this way: "So be careful. If you are thinking, 'Oh, I would never behave like that'— let this be a warning to you. For you too may fall into sin. But remember this—the wrong desires that come into your life aren't anything new and different. Many others have faced exactly the same problems before you . . ." (1 Corinthians 10:12, 13).

The five fiery serpents of lust, idolatry, fornication, tempting God, and murmuring will face all of us in the wilderness of our problems. Everyone will be tempted to think that our personal situation is somehow unique and, therefore, exempt from God's rules and principles. We have read that Paul assures us this isn't so!

One of Satan's most often-used religious questions is the suggestion that God has provided a *situation ethic* for our personal and exceptional case. Adulteries have been committed—money stolen—lies told—and other sins by men and women who rationalized until they deceived themselves into thinking God had made an exception—just for them.

There is no unique situation that provides an exception to the rules in God's dealings with us. The situations have been faced by others, and are known by God.

Paul went on to say, ". . . no temptation is irresistible. You can trust God to keep the temptation from becoming so strong that you can't stand up against it, for he has promised this and will do what he says . . ." (1 Corinthians 10:13).

Temptation is never meant to break us—only to bring out in us what needs to be exposed. We *can* stand up against any temptation (that is a promise) even if the problem appears to be overwhelming. The strength of Christ can take us through to victory.

If things get too rough, we are provided with an escape hatch. Paul concludes with, ". . . He [God] will show you how to escape temptation's power so that you can bear up patiently against it" (v. 13). If we panic, God will come into the problem to rescue us rather than see us fail. But, as a consequence, our time in the wilderness will be extended —because the only way to the promised land is to come *successfully* through the problem on faith in God's Word alone!

If we yield completely to the principle, turning ourselves over to Christ, He will supply the strength to take us through the problem. Remember, He is the one who gained victory *in* temptation. That victory is ours when we are properly related to Him.

11

How to Possess the Land

When the Israelites finally left the wilderness and crossed over the River Jordan into the Promised Land, they faced a reality which many of us, as "spiritual Israelites," tend to forget: The land was still in possession of the enemy! There were enemy nations—giants—and fortified cities in the land! *We may enter the land, but that doesn't mean we are in full possession of it.*

As a young Christian, I used to think that some day "soon" I would come into my promised land and possess it all instantly. Perhaps it would happen in seminary, or at a camp meeting, or a revival, or after prayer with some great man of the faith. I imagined myself transformed into a super-Christian who would never waver, doubt, stumble, or fall —one who would never be tempted to lose patience or to become discouraged under pressure. I expected something to happen inside me and I would experience instant maturity —a man who couldn't do anything wrong!

The Bible tells us that instant possession of the promised land, or instant spiritual maturity, is impossible. This isn't because God isn't capable of giving it to us all at once, but because if He did, we would be destroyed. Listen to Moses as he explains God's plan to the Israelites:

> When the Lord brings you into the Promised Land, as he soon will, he will destroy the following seven nations, all greater and mightier than you . . . No do not be afraid of [them], for the Lord your God is among you . . . He will cast them out a little at the time; he will not do it all at once, for if he did, the wild animals would multiply too quickly and become dangerous.   Deuteronomy 7:1, 21

Our promised land can become ours only a little at a time, too, because we must have time to grow in ability to possess it. *Spectacular and unusually rapid growth in a church, a group, or individual is abnormal.* If you look closely, you may find the "wild animals" there: instability, pure emotionalism, dangerous doctrine, and a lack of solid teaching and faith.

Peter understood the necessity of possessing the land "little by little." He had once thought himself ready to enter the land and possess it all—immediately! The result: he fell flat on his face.

For three years Peter had been a disciple of Jesus. He had been given solid training in the principles of God by the Master Teacher. On the eve of His betrayal, Jesus stated a promise to His followers.

> . . . because you have stood true to me in these terrible days, and because my Father has granted me a Kingdom, I here and now grant you the right to eat and drink at my table in that Kingdom; and you will sit on thrones judging the twelve tribes of Israel.   Luke 22:28–30

Jesus was talking about what is to happen after He returns to earth the second time, but I believe it is also a reference to "reigning in life" in a promised land of today. Immediately after the above startling statement, Jesus continued:

> Simon, Simon [Whenever Jesus called Peter by the name Simon, He was addressing his old, unstable nature. Simon means *wishy-washy*, while Peters means *rock*.] Satan has asked to have you, to sift you like wheat, but I have pleaded in prayer for you that your faith should not completely fail. So, when you have repented and turned to me again, strengthen and build up the faith of your brothers. vs. 31, 32

Jesus permitted Satan to come near Simon because he needed to be exposed to temptation. In his heart was a little something that had to be put to the test before he could enter the promised land as the leader who could strengthen and build up the faith of his brothers. If Peter was to become what Jesus wanted him to be, Jesus had no choice but to expose him to the problem. It is a little frightening to realize that Jesus must do the same with us. We know that He is pleading our cause and praying that our faith won't completely fail us. But Jesus can't pray that we be kept *from* the problem.

In training our children, we can teach them about life and about making choices between right and wrong. But there comes a time when they *must* be exposed to temptation and make the choice on their own. If we insist on making the choices for them, they will never grow up to be mature individuals. As a parent, I have watched my children go into situations where I know they will be tested. I cannot decide the outcome, and I pray that their faith will not fail completely.

Continuing our conversation between Jesus and Peter,

we hear Peter reacting to Jesus' statement in the same way most of us would have responded.

"Lord, I am ready to go to jail with you, and even to die with you."   Luke 22:33

There was a little pride and self-sufficiency in Peter. He was probably thinking, "Lord, what do You mean—pray for me? I don't need it, I'm Your most loyal disciple!" He assumed he was ready for any trial—he felt spiritual, strong, and capable to meet whatever might come along. Listen as Paul, some years later, warns against this attitude:

Therefore let any one who thinks he stands—who feels sure that he has a steadfast mind and is standing firm—take heed lest he fall [into sin].   1 Corinthians 10:12 AMPLIFIED

When we *feel* strong, we no longer depend on Christ for our strength. We forget our need of Him, and immediately begin to stumble. Peter thought he was standing firm and the word *stumble* was not in his vocabulary at the moment. However, Jesus knew what lay ahead and continued:

But Jesus said, "Peter, let me tell you something. Between now and tomorrow morning when the rooster crows, you will deny me three times, declaring that you don't even know me."   Luke 22:34

Peter's reply isn't recorded for us, but I am sure he felt certain that Jesus' prediction would never come true. Peter was eager and anxious to prove his loyalty, and felt ready to go to jail or be killed for his Lord.

It is easy for me to identify with Peter. Often I have wanted to storm out and do something heroic, something exciting—and maybe even dangerous—to further the kingdom. Christians accelerate their "will-power valve" and engage in frantic activities "for the Lord," but that is seldom the way God does things. Some believers may be called to risk their lives on a mission to smuggle Bibles behind the Iron Curtain, but not until they have learned yieldedness and obedience in the small unglamorous things of daily stewardship. We are always anxious to invent our own battles and our own problems. We would do better to wait on the Lord and His command.

Peter wanted an obvious challenge—an outward battle with a recognizable enemy. But Jesus knew his heart, even as He knows ours. Listen as Luke concludes Peter's handling of this problem in verses 56–62. The event followed Jesus' arrest and early morning trial at the residence of the High Priest. Peter had moved into the courtyard. Here a servant girl noticed him in the light of the fire, and said:

"This man was with Jesus!"
Peter denied it. "Woman," he said, "I don't even know the man!"
After a while someone else looked at him and said, "You must be one of them!"
"No sir, I am not!" Peter replied.
About an hour later someone else flatly stated, "I know this fellow is one of Jesus' disciples, for both are from Galilee."
But Peter said, "Man, I don't know what you are talking about."
And as he said the words, a rooster crowed.
At that moment Jesus turned and looked at Peter. Then Peter remembered what he had said—"Before the rooster crows tomorrow morning, you will deny me three times."
And Peter walked out of the courtyard, crying bitterly.

Whenever I read that account I feel as if I'm standing in Peter's shoes, looking into the loving eyes of the Lord. Those eyes held no condemnation, only compassion and understanding. Peter saw himself in those eyes, stripped of all pretense, totally unworthy of his Lord's trust. Yet, he also saw that Jesus had known all along of his weakness, and had loved him.

Peter must have died a thousand deaths that morning, crying tears of repentance, empty of the self that had boasted so brashly of his own strength. Peter had fallen, but his faith had not totally failed. He may have remembered the words from a portion of the Scriptures of his day —and ours—Psalm 37:23, 24:

The steps of good men are directed by the Lord. He delights in each step they take. If they fall it isn't fatal for the Lord holds them with his hand.

Peter was a good man and in his heart was a disposition to do God's will. He didn't perish in the problem, and the temptation had been necessary to expose the pride and self-sufficiency that had to go before Peter could become totally dependent on God.

The old Peter would have wanted to rush in and possess the entire promised land at once. But the new Peter knew the need for steady growth in the faith. He had learned how to strengthen and build up the faith of his brothers so that they would not make the same mistake he had made.

This was part of the preparation necessary to enable Peter to write to the converts of the first century some years later.

Simon Peter, a servant and apostle (special messenger) of Jesus Christ, to those who have received (obtained an equal privilege of) like precious faith with ourselves in *and* through

the righteousness of our God and Savior Jesus Christ: . . .
He has bestowed on us His precious and exceedingly great
promises, so that through them you may escape (by flight)
from the moral decay (rottenness and corruption) that is in
the world because of covetousness (lust and greed), and
become sharers (partakers) of the divine nature.

2 Peter 1:1, 4 AMPLIFIED

This is our promised land and Peter tells us how it is
to be possessed—little by little—as he continues in the above
letter. There are *nine* additives that he lists, saying these
must be cultivated—one by one—to build upon the founda-
tional promise. Thus we shall become partakers of the nature
of Christ.

1. *Diligence:* Be persistent, stick to it, work at it. And remember, it isn't our *own* work, but rather persistence
   in clinging to Christ who works *in* us. Use your diligence to exercise *faith.*
2. *Faith:* Employ every effort to exercise your faith. Settle in
   your heart the essence of faith as given to us in Hebrews 11:1: ". . . faith is the assurance (the confir-
   mation, the title deed) of things [we] hope for, being the proof of things [we] do not see, *and* the con-
   viction of their reality—faith perceiving as real fact
   what is not revealed to the senses" (AMPLIFIED).

   Faith exercised will develop in you *virtue.*
3. *Virtue:* That means doing it right. Don't take the short
   cut! Virtue is excellence, true goodness, uprightness,
   resolution and Christian energy. Practice it to develop
   knowledge.
4. *Knowledge:* Learn to know God better and discover what
   He wants you to do. Seek out His will for you. Study
   your Bible. Don't spend your life being spoon-fed by

others. Get a good Bible dictionary and learn how to use a concordance. Grow up in your personal knowledge of God, His ways and His Word. In practicing what you know about God's ways and wants from you, develop *self-control*.

5. *Self-control:* This is a difficult one! Have you ever promised you won't get mad again? You make this promise to your wife and she reminds you sweetly, "But, honey, you *always* lose your temper." To which you flare back, **"Well, I said I wouldn't do it anymore!"**

What causes us to lose control? Our stubborn self-will. We get mad when *our* will is opposed, *our* comfort disturbed, *our* opinion questioned. The problem is always our giant-sized egos. How can we practice self-control? Not by gritting our teeth and saying, "I won't get mad—I won't get mad." Our self will be controlled when we put aside our own desires, die to our ego, and let Jesus control us. When our self is controlled by Him, we have learned the real meaning of the word. When this happens, you will develop *patience*.

6. *Patience:* This is steadfast endurance in all circumstances and only develops as it is practiced. I have a struggle in this area.

Not too long ago, I took my car to be inspected. The line ahead of me was long, and as I waited I became rather pleased with my own calm steadfastness. I even managed to smile pleasantly when the inspector announced—when I had finally made it— "Reverend, your headlights need adjusting."

Returning to the inspection station, I saw the line had grown considerably—and I noted that my patience was a little frayed around the edges—but I was holding on.

The second time I faced the inspector, the car passed but I was not able to produce my license—I had left it at home! I swallowed bravely and headed for home.

Judy accompanied me on my third attempt. Why does one seem to hit every red light when patience is running low? At one intersection we found ourselves behind a Volkswagen. As the light turned green, the woman at the wheel didn't get her car moving—a second red light—and then a third one. By this time, I was gripping the wheel and thinking seriously about pushing the car through the intersection.

Almost afraid to look as the fourth green light came up, the Volkswagen finally got going and moved slowly ahead. Following a few inches behind her tailgate, sounding my horn, came the once-patient motorist on his way back to the inspection station. The woman looked back at us, smiled, and moved to the side to permit us to pass.

Judy looked at me sideways (as wives have a way of doing) and said sweetly, "Bob, why don't you invite her to our class tonight and teach on patience?"

Patience only comes when you turn your preferences over to Jesus. He can sit through three or four green lights—just as He did in the back of a sinking boat—without getting tense. He is able to reign in all circumstances of life; and when you let Him control you, you will begin to partake of the divine nature and the divine patience. Practicing steadfast patience leads to *godliness*.

7. *Godliness:* This is a word with many implications. An important one is impartiality or justice. God is totally just and impartial. You can measure your godliness by the way you treat your enemies. Do you love them like you do your friends? If you were God and had some rain to give, on whom would you send it? The just *and* the unjust? The ability to be impartial is a mark of godliness. As you practice godliness, you develop *brotherly affection.*

8. *Brotherly affection:* Can you look at every man with compassion? Even if he is dirty, ugly, or mean? Brotherly affection is part of the provision God has made for us. Put aside the old reactions to people you dislike. Yield yourself to Christ and let His affection come through you. He loves all men as brothers. Practicing brotherly affection will develop *Christian love.*

9. *Christian love:* This is the final step on our ladder of preparation to possess the land. Christian love is *agape,* the highest form of love—a reasoning, intentional, deliberate, spiritual devotion for someone. This is not an emotional feeling—variable as the wind—but a steady, unchanging affection.

   The natural love most of us humans are capable of is always directed towards something or someone we like, are attracted to, and approve. Agape is the nature of God's love. He loves us when we are ugly, wrong, and rebellious. Admittedly, it is impossible for us to love like that unless Christ lives and loves in us. With His love in us, we can *will* to love as God directs us, regardless of our feelings.

   When we find ourselves confronted with someone we don't *feel* loving towards, we can confess our lack

of love, resist our human feelings, yield ourselves to
Christ, and ask that He make us able to love.

Agape love makes it possible to experience unfail-
ing love in marriage. No marriage need ever die for
lack of love. If love appears to have cooled, the answer is confession, repentance, and a willingness to
stand on God's principle. The problem may be rough,
but God's provision is secured for us by Christ.

Jesus commanded us to love—even our enemies.
He would not have done so if the provision was not
already available.

Look again at Peter's nine principles. See how they are
linked together progressively. They can only be developed
one by one, *little by little*. We need them to possess the land.
One friend typed these on a card, linking each principle to
the next one with an arrow, and placed the list next to the
bathroom mirror. Each morning provided an opportunity
for check-up. How would you measure up against this reminder?

Peter concludes his thoughts with the following encouragements and promises:

The more you go on in this way, the more you will grow
strong spiritually and become fruitful and useful to our Lord
Jesus Christ. But anyone who fails to go after these additions
to faith is blind indeed, or at least very short-sighted, and
has forgotten that God delivered him from the old life of sin
so that now he can live a strong, good life for the Lord.

2 Peter 1:8–11

Did you notice the encouragements? In the promised land,
we are fruitful and useful to our Lord, and can live a strong,
good life. If we don't go after the additions to the faith Christ

has provided for us, we're short-sighted, wandering in the wilderness, suffering, and stumbling. God's intention is to bring us into the promised land. Anyone who doesn't eagerly accept that opportunity is very foolish, indeed, says Peter.

So, dear brothers, work hard to prove that you are really among those God has called and chosen, and then you will *never stumble or fall away.*   v. 10

The word Peter uses here for *never* means *positively, absolutely, guaranteed never!* Peter knew what it meant to fall, and he learned what it takes to keep from falling. When you have allowed Christ to develop these nine principles in your life, you will never, *ever* fall. There will be nothing in your heart that will cause you to stumble when temptation comes to sift you and prepare you to possess the land.

And God will open wide the gates of heaven [the promised land] for you to enter into the eternal kingdom of our Lord and Savior Jesus Christ.   v. 11

I assure you that that kingdom begins here and now—and waits for us to *enter and possess it—little by little!*

12

Personal Conduct in Battle

When we enter the promised land, we find ourselves face to face with formidable adversaries. They have no intention of relinquishing their possessions without a bitter struggle. God has promised to drive our enemies out before us, little by little, but our participation and personal conduct in the battle will determine the outcome.

Again, our example is the Israelites. The story of how they came to possess their biblical Promised Land, little by little, demonstrates the same principle over and over again: (1) When they obeyed God and trusted Him completely, He always won the battle for them; (2) when they relied on their own strength, they lost. Joshua and Jehoshaphat were two leaders who led their armies to victory by obeying and trusting God.

The story of the Battle of Jericho is told in Joshua, chapter 6. God told Joshua to commandeer his forces and march around the fortified city seven times in seven days. On the last time around, they were to blow their trumpets and the walls would come tumbling down—and they did! Archeologists have dug at the site of old Jericho and found the remains of an old city wall which apparently fell *outward* as the result of an earthquake or other powerful force. What happened at Jericho is verifiable fact, not an old myth or fairy tale.

Later, Jehoshaphat and his men faced the multitudes of the armies of Moab, Ammon, and Mount Seit. But God told them:

> . . . Don't be afraid! Don't be paralyzed by this mighty army! For the battle isn't yours, but God's!
>
> 2 Chronicles 20:15

We read that God instructed Jehoshaphat to place his band of singers and musicians in full view of the enemy forces, and while they sang praises to Jehovah, He turned the enemy armies against each other until they had completely destroyed each other. The Israelites didn't receive a scratch.

The battle was God's, but the outcome depended on the conduct of the Israelites during the fighting. Had they doubted God's word and involved themselves in the fighting, He could not have kept them from harm. *God can only fight our battles if we follow His instructions and trust Him for the outcome.*

Our preparation for the battles God has promised to win for us consists of learning to get our own selves out of the way so that we can rely totally on God.

As we look back over the wilderness, over the problems and the temptations, we recognize that it is all part of the preparation for the battles to possess the promised land.

When the young army recruit first comes to boot camp,

he's half-scared because he doesn't know what is expected of him. He gets his verbal and written instructions first. Then come the exercises to develop his physical endurance, his ability to handle weapons, and to conduct himself under simulated battle conditions. By the time he is through with training, he's eager to see some action and test in practice the principles he has been taught.

The young Christian is a recruit in the army of the Lord. The terminology of warfare is much used throughout the Bible to emphasize the very real battle between the forces of good and evil in our world. The Christian life is to be on the front lines, although the battle isn't ours—but God's.

Our preparations for battle start with the verbal and written instructions from God's Word. We need to know what is expected of us, and how God works. Then the rough part of the training comes when we move into problems and temptations to develop our endurance and test what we have learned.

God continues to offer opportunities for growth. He feeds us and strengthens us daily with His Word. Whenever we are presented with fresh teaching and messages, we should

be on the alert to drink them in and make them a part of our equipment, for we may be certain that we are going to need it as we move forward to battle. When we understand the principle and know what is expected of us, we can move with eager anticipation into the subsequent phases of our training.

The Apostle James experienced the joy of being prepared for battle in his day. He shares this word with us:

> Consider it wholly joyful, my brethren, whenever you are enveloped in *or* encounter trials of any sort *or* fall into various temptations.   James 1:2 AMPLIFIED

> . . . for when the way is rough, your patience has a chance to grow. So let it grow and don't try to squirm out of your problems. For when your patience is finally in full bloom, then you will be ready for anything, strong in character, full and complete.   vs. 3, 4 LB

We are ready for battle when we have gone through problems and temptations that have stripped us of our self-dependency and taught us to depend solely on God for strength.

Another of the apostles of the Early Church, Paul, left us some challenging words on battle preparation.

> . . . I want to remind you that your strength must come from the Lord's mighty power within you. Put on all of God's armor so that you will be able to stand safe againt all strategies and tricks of Satan. For we are not fighting against people made of flesh and blood, but against persons without bodies—the evil rulers of the unseen world, those mighty satanic beings and great evil princes of darkness who rule this world; and against huge numbers of wicked spirits in the spirit world.   Ephesians 6:10–12

A few years ago, most Christians in our western "civilized" world thought Paul expressed the unenlightened and superstitious beliefs of his age when he described our enemies as "mighty satanic beings, great evil princes of darkness and wicked spirits." Today we are seeing increasing evidence of how real the powers of darkness are, and what formidable enemies they can be. Those who have fought the desperate battles against drug addiction, alcoholism, or homosexuality, to mention only three areas where the powers of darkness are at work, have discovered that it is impossible to be victorious in their own strength. If these battles are to be won at all, they must be won by God.

The forces of darkness are actively at work in rebellion, crime, marriage breakups, sickness, and many other ills from which we suffer. But here, as in temptation, *the outcome hangs in the delicate balance between the individual, God, and the forces of evil.* Jesus Christ has already won the battle for us. Satan is defeated. But in each situation, the outcome depends on personal response. If one chooses to resist evil and yield totally to God, He will fight and win the battles for us.

Paul has some further advice for us with some specifics for getting ready to meet the enemy.

So use every piece of God's armor [Don't use any of your own] to resist the enemy whenever he attacks, and when it is all over, you will be standing up. [The Greek word Paul used for *standing* is a military term, meaning to stand as a conqueror]. But to do this, you will need the strong belt of truth and the breastplate of God's approval. Wear the shoes that are able to speed you on as you preach the Good News of peace with God. In every battle you will need faith as your shield to stop the fiery arrows aimed at

you by Satan. And you will need the helmet of salvation
and the sword of the Spirit—which is the Word of God.
Ephesians 6:13–16

Everything we need to stand in the battle is provided for
us. We don't have to be clever or strong or superspiritual.
We only need to rely on Jesus Christ. Be happy when you
find yourself moving into a battle, because the outcome will
reveal one of two things: If you stand, it shows that you
have absorbed what you need of the Christ-life to receive
your provision of victory; if you fall, you can be happy, as
well—because the battle has revealed what is really in your
heart and what you need for facing the next battle! It is a
great deal better to discover any weaknesses so that they
may be adjusted, rather than to have it revealed in eternity!
If there is anger, resentment, or pride in your heart, and this
is keeping you from claiming your rightful possession of the
promised land—wouldn't you rather find out about it now?

God allowed Joshua to lose a battle in order to show him
that there was a hidden sin in his camp. Once that sin was
exposed and removed, God led Joshua into battle with the
same enemy and gave him victory. The story is recorded in
Joshua, chapters 7 and 8.

After the battle at Jericho, God gave the Israelites specific
instructions not to keep any battle loot for themselves. One
of Joshua's men, Achan, couldn't resist a beautiful robe, stole
it, and hid it in the ground under his tent.

Later Joshua sent some of his men to spy on the city of
Ai. They returned with the report that it was a small city
and wouldn't take more than two or three thousand of them
to destroy it. In fact, they said, ". . . there's no point in all
of us going there" (Joshua 7:4).

The Israelites, confident after their easy victory at Jericho, marched up against Ai, ". . . and they were soundly defeated . . . The Israeli army was paralyzed with fear at this turn of events. Joshua and the elders tore their clothing and lay prostrate before the Ark of the Lord until evening, with dust on their heads" (vs. 4–6).

Joshua had gone into battle unaware of the hidden sin in his camp. But he had also made a mistake himself. He had neglected to consult God before going up against this new enemy. If we turn to God *before* a battle and pray, "Lord, let there not be any hidden sin in me that will cause You to have to lead me into temptation—reveal that hidden sin now," then God is able to show us any trouble point without putting us through a losing battle.

Realizing immediately that God had permitted the defeat in order to show him something, Joshua turned in repentance and God told him about Achan's sin. The culprit was brought into the open and he and his entire family destroyed. Then God said to Joshua:

> . . . Don't be afraid or discouraged; take the entire army and go to Ai, for it is now yours to conquer. I have given the king of Ai and all his people to you. You shall do to them as you did to Jericho and her king, but this time you may keep the loot and the cattle for yourselves. . . .
>
> Joshua 8:1, 2

Why had God made the ruling against taking loot at Jericho? Because He knew the weakness, spirit of disobedience, and greed in Achan. He permitted the temptation to bring the weakness out into the open. Once the weakness was exposed and repented of, God told Joshua not to be discouraged or afraid.

When we suffer defeat in battle, we should realize that

God permits it to show us a weakness which He wants to replace with His strength. We should not be discouraged or
afraid, for God never reveals our weakness in order to con-
demn us. He simply gives us opportunity to rid ourselves of
our old nature so that we may replace it with the divine
nature He has promised us.

Therefore, we can rejoice in our defeats and failures,
knowing that the ultimate end God desires for us is good. I
have often learned as much (if not more) from a failure as
from a success.

Defeats serve as a reminder (as it did in the case of Joshua
and his men) that all is not well in our camp. We may roll
along fairly smoothly, oblivious to our own tendencies to
self-willed rebellion, until we stumble and fall in a battle.
We should thank God right then and there for reminding us
that we need Him. A defeat or failure is designed to bring
us back to God. If we are not certain what caused the
trouble, we must say as David did:

Search me, O God, and know my heart; test my thoughts.
Point out anything you find in me that makes you sad, and
lead me along the path of everlasting life. Psalms 139:23, 24

First, we must return to God; second, we must confess
that we are at fault. Even when we do not know our specific
mistake, we must, like Joshua, repent. For we know that if
we had followed given instructions and relied totally on the
life and strength of Christ, victory would have been as-
sured. Christ cannot fail. When we fail, it is because of our
wrongdoing at some point.

Repentance leads to renewal. Hear David as he prayed
following his discovery of wrongdoing.

I admit my shameful deed—it haunts me day and night . . .
You saw it all and your sentence against me is just . . .
Sprinkle me with the cleansing blood and I shall be clean
again. Wash me and I shall be whiter than snow. And after
you have punished me [after my defeat], give me back my
joy again . . . Create in me a new, clean heart. . . . O God,
filled with clean thoughts and right desires.   Psalms 51:3–10

A clean heart and a new nature is part of the promised
land. Little by little God exposes and renews our hearts. We
couldn't take a complete overhaul at once. One by one, the
compartments where there is selfishness—fear—greed—lust
—idolatry—jealousy and other trouble spots, will be brought
out into the open, cleansed, and renewed. This gives place
to the new nature—love—joy—peace—kindness—patience—
goodness—faithfulness—and self-control!

Look at your failures as opportunities for growth, bringing you closer to God. Pick yourself up and say, "Sorry I
missed it again, Lord. Show me—teach me—change me." As
we learn to trust ourselves less and Christ more; and as we
learn to come to Him *before* the battle starts, we can be as-
sured of increasing victories.

God will give us wisdom if we ask for it. He wants us to
go into battle fully prepared as to how to conduct ourselves . . . .

If you want to know what God wants you to do, ask him and
he will gladly tell you, for he is always ready to give a
bountiful supply of wisdom to all who ask him. He will not
resent it. But when you ask him, be sure that you really
expect him to tell you, for a doubtful mind will be as un-
settled as a wave of the sea that is driven and tossed by the
wind; and every decision you then make will be uncertain,
as you turn first this way and then that. If you don't ask

> with faith, don't expect the Lord to give you any solid
> answer.   James 1:5–8

What could be more specific than these words? When we
have learned how to turn the promise of wisdom into provision, we can come to God and say, "Lord, I see I am getting
into a battle. I don't want to squirm out of it. I want to go
through it in Your strength and I want You to tell me how
to conduct myself while I am in the problem." God will give
us wisdom when we ask for it. That is a provision.

But, we must apply the principle of faith through the
problem. We must *believe* that God can and will supply the
wisdom. The problem will present us with the temptation
to doubt and waver, and the outcome will be decided by us.
We must resist the doubting and wavering and yield ourselves to Him who can supply the faith to take us through to
provision and victory.

After victory in the battle we will reign as kings in life.

> Happy is the man who doesn't give in and do wrong when
> he is tempted, for afterwards he will get as his reward
> the crown of life that God promised those who love him.
>   James 1:12

The provision is ours—the promised land with cities we
didn't build—wells we didn't dig—and orchards we didn't
plant. There we are to experience financial security—marital
joy—resting in God's care. This is the place of rest where we
can do all things through Christ who strengthens us. There
will be enemies and problems, but we are reigning over
them in the peace and strength Christ affords.

Not long ago, a phone call came to my office. Our four-
year-old son had been taken to the emergency room at the

hospital. Rushing there, I found my wife Judy at his bedside. He had been struck by a car while playing outside our home, and had received cuts, bruises, and a fractured femur at the base of the pelvis.

As we stood by his bedside, the *temptation* came to feel that we were being punished by God. Instead, Judy and I were both swept with joy and an awareness of God's tremendous love for us and our little boy. Standing in the emergency room with hands raised before the Lord in gratitude, we came to understand what it means to "consider it wholly joyful . . . whenever you are enveloped in *or* encounter trials of any sort *or* fall into various temptations" (James 1:2 AMPLIFIED). The wonderful provision from Romans chapter 8 was ours.

Who can then keep Christ's love from us? When we have trouble or calamity, when our little boy is hit by a car and seriously injured? *No nothing* will ever be able to separate us from the love of God demonstrated by our Lord Jesus Christ when he died for us. This is *provision*—and it is ours to claim!

As Christians and spiritual Israelites, we are not meant to be permanant wilderness-wanderers. God wants us to lay claim to the provisions provided for us in our promised land. He wants us to recognize *why* He led us into the wilderness and *where* He wants to take us.

Have you learned to identify the promise, the principle, and the problem?

Have you come to see the purpose of temptation and the religious question?

Do you understand that if we fail once or twice—or even three times—in the problem, we know we can pick ourselves up and take another lap around the mountain without feeling guilty about it?

Do you know where to turn for instructions when you are in doubt about the reason for your failure?

Have you come to realize that when you do stand and enter the promised land, that there will be battles yet before you?

Do you feel more thoroughly prepared to wait for God to give instructions for enemy attack and drive the invaders out before you?

Can you meet with wilderness experiences, with their problems, temptations, and religious questions, with the assurance that these are not given to keep us from our provisions—but to prepare us to receive them?

As you answer these questions, I pray that this book will have helped you to count it joy when trials and temptations come—because you now understand that God's purpose in temptation is to move you into your promised land where His provisions are rightfully yours. May you never resign yourself to a life of permanent defeat but be strong in battle for claiming His promises!

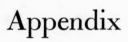

Appendix

APPENDIX 21 WILDERNESSES IN THE BIBLE—The Four *Ps* Illustrated

		Promise	Principle	Problem	Provision
1	Adam and Eve Genesis 2, 3	Fellowship with God, the Garden of Eden	Obedience to God's command	Satanic temptation	Failed
2	Abraham Genesis 12–22	Father of nations	Faith and obedience	Years of waiting, laps in problem	"Father of the Faith"
3	Isaac Genesis 25	Promised a son	Willingness and obedience	Twenty years childless	Birth of Jacob and Esau
4	Jacob Genesis 29	Marriage to Rachel	Obedience to Laban	Deception and injustice	Rachel as bride
5	Joseph Genesis 37–45	Dream of greatness	Faith and obedience	Sold into slavery, jail and suffering	Rescued his people from famine
6	Moses Exodus 2–14	To deliver his people	Faith and obedience	Kills Egyptian, years in exile	Delivers his people from Egypt
7	Israel Exodus, Leviticus, Numbers, Deuteronomy	The Promised Land	Willingness and obedience	Forty years in wilderness	First generation failed
8	Job Job	Perfection of faith	Trust and obedience	Spiritual and physical testing	Faith, abundant restoration
9	David 1 Samuel 16–31	To be king	Obedience to will of God	Persecution by Saul in wilderness	Anointed king
10	Every Man Psalm 23	Cup running over, anointing	Faith in Good Shepherd	Valley of death	Eternal blessings

		Marriage to the King	Willingness to follow King	Wilderness experiences	Belonging to the Beloved
11	Maiden Song of Solomon				Belonging to the Beloved
12	Messiah Isaiah 52 and 53	Shall be exalted	Obedience to will of God	Despised, rejected, grief, and sorrow	Receive a portion with the great
13	Christ Luke 4	Saviour	Obedience to God's Word	Temptation in wilderness	Messianic fullness
14	Mary Luke 1	Mother of our Lord	Faith and obedience	Humiliation, misunderstanding	Honor and recognition
15	Peter Luke 22	Keys to Kingdom	Submission and faith	Denial of his Lord	Restored and established
16	Disciples Luke 24	Authority and witness	Stability in faith	Crucifixion of Christ	Meeting the resurrected Christ
17	N. T. church Acts 20	Preach pure gospel of repentance and faith in Christ	Hold fast to pure doctrine	Division, grievous wolves	Inheritance of those who are set apart (*see v. 32*)
18	Paul Philippians 1	Apostle of Jesus Christ	Faith, obedience and humility	Persecution, beatings, prison, suffering	Prize of his high calling of God in Christ (*see Philippians 3:14*)
19	Timothy 1 and 2 Timothy	Usefulness in God's work	Faith, diligence, obedience	Spiritual warfare, false teachers	Strength and boldness, full provision
20	Christian life Galatians 2: 20	Freedom from bondage	Christ in us	Dying to self	Resurrection life
21	Believers Romans 5–8	Reign in life (Romans 5)	Dead to self, risen with Christ (Romans 6)	Conflict between old and new nature (Romans 7)	The promised land (Romans 8)

This book is adapted from the popular tape series: THE PURPOSE AND PRINCIPLE OF TEMPTATION, which is accompanied by an illustrated study guide to aid in group study.

This series is available from

Bob Mumford
Box 22341
Fort Lauderdale, Florida   33315